Reading Marx

Reading Marx

Slavoj Žižek, Frank Ruda, and
Agon Hamza

polity

First published in 2018 by Polity Press

Polity Press
65 Bridge Street
Cambridge CB2 1UR, UK

Polity Press
101 Station Landing
Suite 300
Medford, MA 02155, USA

ISBN-13: 978-1-5095-2140-1
ISBN-13: 978-1-5095-2141-8(pb)

A catalogue record for this book is available from the British Library.

Library of Congress Cataloging-in-Publication Data

Names: Zizek, Slavoj, author.
Title: Reading Marx / Slavoj Zizek, Frank Ruda, Agon Hamza.
Description: Medford, MA : Polity, 2018. | Includes bibliographical references and index.
Identifiers: LCCN 2017053287 (print) | LCCN 2018002710 (ebook) | ISBN 9781509521449 (Epub) | ISBN 9781509521401 (hardback) | ISBN 9781509521418 (pbk.)
Subjects: LCSH: Marx, Karl, 1818-1883.
Classification: LCC B3305.M74 (ebook) | LCC B3305.M74 Z59 2018 (print) | DDC 335.4092--dc23
LC record available at https://lccn.loc.gov/2017053287

Typeset in 11 on 14 pt Utopia by
Servis Filmsetting Ltd, Stockport, Cheshire
Printed and bound in Great Britain by CPI Group (UK) Ltd, Croydon

For further information on Polity, visit our website: politybooks.com

Contents

Notes on the text

The first chapter, *Marx Reads Object-Oriented Ontology*, was written by Slavoj Žižek, the second chapter, *Marx in the Cave*, by Frank Ruda, and the third, *Imprinting Negativity: Hegel Reads Marx*, by Agon Hamza. The introduction and conclusion are coauthored.

Introduction
Unexpected Reunions

This book is written by three philosophers. Its aim is to find different (and yet unexplored) ways to read Marx. This collective project dedicated to Marx's work (*Capital* being one of its primary sources, though by no means the only one) is situated within the specific philosophical and political conjuncture in which we find ourselves. It is, indeed, a peculiar, situation, though not entirely unique. To demonstrate its peculiarity as well as its uniqueness, let us take a quick look at the fairly "short history" of Marxism and communism. Marxism has a "short" history in comparison to other histories, such as the victorious history of democracy, whose flawed political form in its infancy – excluding women and slaves in ancient Greece – took much longer to actualize than one usually likes to remember. If we look back at previous historical situations and the state of "Marxism" or "communism" within them, we can recognize certain similarities with the present one. Similarities, because conceiving of emancipation (or revolution) within these historical configurations seemed almost as impossible

1

then as it does today (maybe even more so, if impossibility knows degrees).

From a Marxist perspective on the history of Marxism, we can therefore immediately learn that such impossibilities (for example, of emancipation) are not strictly ontological, but are always historically determined and thus specific. The impossibility of conceiving of an overall transformation of a given political system is not simply conceptual, but is also determined by a concrete historical situation; it hinges on a specific articulation of particular points of impossibility. From a Marxist perspective on the history of Marxism, modal categories show their historical face. But this is not all we can learn from such a perspective. We can also learn that the practices gathered under the name of "Marxism" or "communism" often implied the conversion of a historically specific impossibility into a new possibility (of emancipation); a modal transformation that also always implied a kind of self-affirmation, a *Selbstbehauptung*, of Marxism itself, of its central assumptions, its axioms. Just think of the claim that there could be a different organization of society, which had first to be established and then found a historical referent in the Paris Commune, which was then taken as the starting point for transformations in Russia.

But, as many others – non-Marxists – have later claimed, from the history of Marxism one can also, and should, ultimately learn that converting what previously appeared to be impossible into a new possibility comes at the high price not only of tolerating violence and creating suffering for millions, including unspeakable injustices, but also of producing new structural impossibilities – or, simply displacing previous ones. So, what appeared to be a practical conversion, from such a perspective, demonstrates that precisely such impossibilities should be left untouched, as it will otherwise only result in a catastrophe.

So, where do we stand today? What is our position in terms of this history?

First, the year 2017 marked the 150th anniversary of the publication of Marx's first volume of *Capital*. This historical fact in itself raises a series of questions (about the philosophical, ideological, epistemological, political, and potential validity and relevance, etc., of Marx's thought), which are determining for as well as determined by the coordinates of our present situation and the history from which it originated. These questions are directly as well as indirectly addressed in this book. What you are about to read is thus not a celebration or unconditional defense of Marx; nor is it an attempt to dissect what is living and what is dead in Marx's thought – in the way that Bernedetto Croce once infamously sought to divide Hegel's philosophy into contemporarily relevant and irrelevant parts. Rather, what you can expect is an attempt to read and thus think with Marx as a contemporary.

Second, our common belief is that even in the present philosophical and political conjuncture, there is a conceptual need that is yet to be determined. A need for Marx – to paraphrase the early Hegel's famous formula of a "need for philosophy" – a need to compel us to return to Marx's oeuvre. Yet, we assume that this return, at this point in history, can only be of a philosophical nature. One might even say that the need for philosophy is directly related to the need for Marx. Why? The present historical situation is generally perceived as one in which we can observe an increasing closure of possibilities and of practical initiatives for emancipation; one can see everywhere a blatant regression to previous forms of domination and use of political power that for long seemed to have been invalidated by history but today returns with a vengeance. Think of the rise of new authoritarian modes of politics, including both "populist" nationalist movements and parties, and even more authoritarian forms of exploitation and value production – the infamous capitalism with Asian values (which after all has nothing to do with Asia as such), which seems to undo what Fukuyama assumed to be the end of history, namely the linkage of democracy and capitalism – including what may have appeared historically abandoned forms of exploitation such as slavery, etc. Yet, if this need for Marx today is located in a conjuncture that is also determined by the history of Marxism, one cannot properly understand it without also taking into account the peculiar fate that Marx's thought has lived through.

On one side, he has been declared dead several times; sometimes he seemed buried under the charge of being one of the – if not the – ultimate culprit(s) for all the victims that the history of Marxism brought about. On the other side, as was already diagnosed by Lenin in 1917, "all the social chauvinists" – Lenin's name for reactionaries who present themselves as emancipators – "are now Marxists (don't laugh!)."[1] "Marx" became the target of operations that suspend the radicality of what was once linked to it. Lenin describes this in the following manner:

> After their deaths attempts are made to convert them into harmless icons, to canonize them, so to speak, and to hallow their *names* to a certain extent for the "consolation" of the

oppressed classes and with the object of duping the latter, while at the same time robbing the revolutionary theory of its *substance*, blunting its revolutionary edge, and vulgarizing it.[2]

Without its revolutionary edge, Marx becomes canonized, a sacred name – and the sacred was always in opposition to the profane, that which is exempted from practical usage.[3] "Marx" became "Saint Marx" (to use one of the polemical nominations that Marx and Engels themselves employed in their *Holy Family*). This canonizing transformation of "Marx" into "Saint Marx" detaches his name from any relation to the present situation. Such a detachment only works by suspending certain elements, certain contents constitutively linked to this name, and thus relies on specific operations of displacement: one "push[es] to the foreground and extol[s] what is or seems acceptable to the bourgeoisie."[4] The acceptable elements of Marx's thought stand in the foreground and thereby cast long shadows on what still seems unacceptable, exaggerated, brazen, or simply too revolutionary in his thought. The transformation of "Marx" into "Saint Marx" consequentially manifested itself in the form of a harmless idolatry that, for Lenin, enabled the gathering of political groups around his name that have no real connection whatsoever to the idea of emancipation or revolution. Even though some of them whole-heartedly demand change, they actually do whatever they can to prevent any proper change from occurring. Lenin describes this assimilation of Marx by means of sacralization by recourse to different operations: "they omit, obscure, and distort"[5] the thought of Marx; it is a "doctoring of Marxism"[6] into what seems convenient.

For example, some "replaced the class struggle with dreams of class harmony" and thereby "even [grew] out of the habit of thinking about proletarian revolution."[7] Anyone was able to be a Marxist, on the basis of forgetting, obscuring, and distorting what it meant to be a Marxist. Lenin provides a detailed list of the specific operations involved in doctoring Marx(ism): for example, repression, distortion, omittance, "amelioration," denial, the cover-up, simplification, betrayal, vulgarization, evasion, disregard, malapropism. All of them alone, but, even more, all of them together, generated a more subtle practice of assimilating resistance to Marx(ism) than any direct rejection or attack ever could; obscure and reactive subjects simply reappropriate the very name representing emancipation. Marx was thereby effectively transformed into a harmless idol that can be easily adored as he is an ineffective, impotent tin god (with "Engels" as his accompanying weak "angel"). Such an idol, distorted and misrepresented, therefore enters the field of history without its revolutionary (conceptual) hammer. For Lenin, such a historical situation raises the question of how to remain faithful to Marx at a time when Marxism is being misrepresented – which is why *State and Revolution* seeks to undertake the project of re-establishing the truth of Marxism, returning to its fundamental principles (which for Lenin is condensed not in class struggle, as one might assume, but in the dictatorship of the proletariat). In short, he undertakes a de-sacralization, a profanation of "Marx," which again can only be realized if one depicts the specific contemporary relevance of Marx's thought on the basis of the concrete historical situation. The truth of Marx's name can only be restored if it becomes effective as a truth of this specific concrete and singularly historical situation, and not simply as a transhistorical dogmatic canonical corpus – or the latter only as being part of the former. This means not judging the validity of Marx from the perspective of the historical situation, but demonstrating the validity of a Marxist perspective for a singular historical situation. The principle is thus not what Marx is as seen through the eyes of the situation, but what the situation is as seen through the eyes of Marx.

One can indeed be tempted to see a contemporary relevance in Lenin's diagnosis, since although "Marx" today is generally considered to be "old hat," even conservatives increasingly tend to agree with him. How is this possible, given that they would certainly not consider themselves to be revolutionary Marxists (or Leninists, etc.)? Often, the answer is that they take Marx's economic analyses to be correct and convincing, but also assume that the political consequences that classical Marxists draw from them are fundamentally misguided.[8] Marx's peculiar fate does not seem to have ended. His theoretical position, having been dogmatically tamed in the form of an official state doctrine, and after having apparently withered away with the previously "really existing socialist (Marxist) states," has become an object of scientific and academic study and is even of interest and relevance to those who previously might have appeared to be class enemies, but with no interest whatsoever in an emancipatory political theory and revolutionary practice.

One might also compare the present state of affairs with the situation in the 1960s, when Marxism was still an integral and constitutive element of philosophical, political, and cultural debate, an element whose relevance and scope were also supposed to be constantly reassigned within, and through, the historical practice and debates that reflected on and directed it. This is no longer the case. If the previous century was a period, generally speaking, that operated under the assumption that history is potentially open, that there are political possibilities – even if they have to be located first and their true potential analyzed later (revolutions, student uprisings, anticolonial struggles, emancipation of women, etc.) – in the present era, Marx (Marxism) seems to have lost this link to concrete practices. We seem to be living through a time in which what was constitutive of historical temporality proper before seems now to be absent (and its "motor" is often simply identified with the dynamics of the capitalist system itself). Today, there are no great political mass events (even though what was referred to as the "Arab Spring" came with the promise of a potential reawakening of history[9]) and previous mass events appear to have no lasting effect at all (their actual consequences, if they are not deemed to be straightforwardly disastrous, are obscure, at least in what concerns their contemporary impact – and this even pertains to the very concept of revolution). If, before, people were forced to keep their respective political, conceptual, and philosophical imaginations up to date with the events that they were experiencing, or even actively participating in, today we live in a historical situation, in which, broadly speaking, the present situation confronts us not only with an increasing closure of possibilities, conceptual means, and initiatives to even conceive of and think about emancipation, but also with an absence of those kinds of practices that force us to think (differently) and (re-)model our practical as well as our theoretical tools and means. As the famous saying goes: it is easier to imagine a comet hitting the earth than it is to envisage even the tiniest transformation in the workings of the capitalist system. This is the doxa that seems to adhere even to the many positions that claim to oppose this very system.

Already, Marxists of the twentieth century were aware that things were developing so rapidly that it was very difficult to keep the conceptual imagination up to date, as the unfolding of events and the reactions to them constantly forced them to think again (about how to continue, what to do, etc.). But, today, there is quite a peculiar regressive development that points in another direction: the reign of reaction, and regressive and obscurantist tendencies. Contrary to the optimism of the Marxists of the twentieth century (especially in the 1960s), we argue that the steam of developments will not result in a rise of the working class or the destruction of the system of domination constitutive of the present world, unavoidably culminating in socialism (as everyone today knows).

The assumption that there is a latent subject of the future revolution that just has to be located and mobilized properly seems to have been one of the greatest limitations of classical Marxism, especially at a time when the dynamics of capitalism are manifested in a form of social organization in which those who are excluded are no longer even exploited by the system; instead, they are kept outside of it, hindered from entering by new walls built practically everywhere: the slum dwellers, the refugees, and all those referred to by Hegel as the poor rabble.[10] The limit, and also the truth, of the contemporary world as it is (which is, no matter how globalized it may be, therefore no longer a proper world, as Alain Badiou has argued), is indeed a reactualized form of barbarism. The famous and previous structural dichotomy of "socialism or barbarism" appears to be suspended today, after alternating between "(capitalist) barbarism or (socialist) barbarism," leaving us with the tautological choice between "(capitalist) barbarism or (barbaric) capitalism" – the only game in town.

We therefore assume that, today, reading Marx carries a specifically philosophical significance. Are there still resources to be extracted from Marx, not only against previous forms of Marxism, but to depict an emancipatory orientation that can show itself to be in line with the present historical conjuncture? How does one read Marx to answer this question? Slavoj Žižek opens his chapter in this book with a claim that is the paradigmatic premise of our reading of Marx: what we need in our contemporary situation is not necessarily a direct reading of his work, but an imagined, inventive, and experimental reading. That is to say, we need to read Marx in such a way that we can imagine how he would have answered those of his critics who have declared him dead or tamed him by over-embracing a doctored Marxist position, and who are seeking to replace him by or even make him compatible with theories of a profoundly different political and ontological orientation. Such a reading maneuver can also necessitate confronting Marx with theoretical positions and conceptual themes from the history of emancipatory thought that at first sight might seem foreign to classical Marxism, as the chapters by Frank Ruda and Agon Hamza demonstrate. Ruda examines what becomes of Marx's depiction of the very constitution of a paradigm of capitalist subjectivity (the worker) if it is read against the background of one of the oldest myths of emancipation (from all myths), namely Plato's cave allegory. Hamza takes the cue from Hegel's theory of labor, for whom work is an activity that imprints negativity in the work itself. In doing so, he aims to model a Marxist theory of labor that exceeds the distinction of abstract and concrete labor and investigates what this means for an understanding of Marxism.

These three chapters can be located against a certain historical and political background of a series of different readings of *Capital*. Hamza has argued elsewhere that there are Marxists who read *Capital* especially in the light of the famous line from the *Manifesto*: "capitalism produces its own gravediggers" – for them, a crisis *in* capitalism is a crisis *of* capitalism, so that it produces the tools for overcoming itself. For others, *Capital* is read in light of another statement from the *Manifesto*, the one about the permanent social revolution brought about by the bourgeoisie – for them, a crisis is a moment of the perpetual internal revolution of capitalism, part of its self-reproduction. Which option is more convincing? Perhaps neither. The much more frightening realization we have come to grasp is that capitalism does in fact reproduce its own logic indefinitely and it does reach an immanent limit. But this limit is not socialism or communism; it is (a regression to) barbarism: the utter destruction of natural and social substance in a "downward spiral" that does not recognize any "reality testing" in this destruction. In this sense, the "gravediggers" that capitalism produces are gravediggers of all alternatives, of the last grains of potential freedom, etc. – which is why no emancipatory project should count on the immanent logic of capitalism to point a way out or wait for its collapse in the hope that we will not be dragged along with it.[11]

As stated, we will read Marx as philosophers. This cannot but remind us of Louis Althusser's proposition from *Reading Capital*. He and his collaborators "read *Capital* as philosophers," a reading fundamentally different from those carried out by economists, historians, and philologists before.[12] And we should add: we do not read *Capital* (merely) as a political book. What we are concerned with is not the status that Marx's critique of political economy occupies in the general history of sciences, nor its immediate relevance for current economic analysis; and we are not reading Marx and his *Capital* as a politico-historical document, since it seems to offer no immediately viable contemporary political "program" to be put into practice.

Althusser and his students carried out a symptomatic reading of Marx's *Capital*. He declared: "There is no such thing as an innocent reading, we must say what reading we are guilty of." By reading *Capital* to the letter and applying the methodology of symptomatic reading, according to Althusser, we can reach and understand the repressed essence of the text – there are always two texts in one text – that which is latent and can become apparent through such a reading. Thus, we can problematize and reconstruct the, as it were, unconscious of the text itself. Althusser goes as far as to see the existence of Marxist philosophy as being conditioned by this form of reading, because through it the concepts and its philosophy can be rendered explicit and "establish the indispensable minimum for the consistent existence" of it; starting from divulging the symptom of a given relation or of a given text.

Althusser and his group of collaborators set out a project of creating the philosophical foundations of reading Marx's *Capital*. It is no wonder that *Reading Capital* opens with his essay, "From Capital to Marx's Philosophy." Its title indeed encapsulates best the goals and paths of the entire project. Departing from Spinoza, the reading of Marx's *Capital* was performed on epistemological grounds. Roughly put, Althusser was concerned with the question "of its relation to its object, hence both the question of the specificity of its object, and the question of the specificity of its relation to that object."[13] Philosophy operates in the field of knowledge and ensures its (re)production. It exists in the field of knowledge alone, preoccupied with and thinking the effects of knowledge on its own terrain.

In the work of Althusser, Marx's *Capital* occupies a very peculiar position. It differs from the "classic economists" not only at the level of object and method;[14] it also presents an "epistemological mutation," thus inaugurating a new object, method, and theory. It is because of this that Althusser takes the very daring step of asking the following question (in the form of a thesis): "Does *Capital* represent the founding moment of a new discipline, the founding moment of a science – and hence a real event, a theoretical revolution, simultaneously rejecting the classical political economy and the Hegelian and Feuerbachian ideologies of its prehistory – the absolute beginning of the history of a science?"[15] In Althusser's understanding of science – concerning which the authors of this book have some conceptual reservations – Marx's discovery is about the opening of a new scientific continent, that of the science of history, which, seen from within the history of sciences, is comparable to two other such discoveries: the unveiling of the continent of mathematics (by the Greeks), and the discovery of the continent of physics (by

Galileo). The opening up of the new continent of science presupposes a "change of a terrain," or, to formulate it in more familiar terms, it presupposes an epistemological break. Every great scientific discovery – and for Althusser the discovery of the science of history is "the most important theoretical event of contemporary history" – involves a great transformation of philosophy. This was the case with mathematics and Plato (the birth of philosophy), physics and Descartes (the beginning of modern philosophy), and the science of history and Marx. The new practice of philosophy, which was inaugurated with the 11th Thesis on Feuerbach, marks the end of classical philosophy. However, Marxist philosophy – that is, dialectical materialism – always comes too late, it is always behind the history of science, that is, historical materialism. Althusser also maintains that apart from lagging behind the sciences, philosophy always comes after politics. But, because *Capital* is, in the last instance according to Althusser, the foundation or "the absolute beginning" of the history of sciences, it is a work of its own history, thus marking a break with the knowledge of modern economics, of political economy. Conceptualizing it as such, by means of a symptomatic reading, Althusser and his collaborators read *Capital* from an epistemological position and attempted to draw on mostly epistemological implications of a philosophical reading, in which they placed *Capital*.

Unlike Althusser's collective endeavor, this book is neither a follow-up and product of a seminar on Marx, *Capital*, and the critique of political economy (it did not originate from any common engagement in a university), nor is it the product of a secretive philosophical cell (that might be comparable to Althusser's "Spinoza circle"). We also do not want to propagate the discovery of a new scientific terrain that Marx's mind and feet touched first. Our approach to Marx and to the critique of political economy is much more partial or engaged. We experimentally attempt to raise the question not of what can be practically done with Marx today, but of what can and what needs to be philosophically (re-) thought – and to examine what are productive (and what are unproductive) tools for doing so. This will not lead us to offer a comprehensive philosophical outline for reading Marx in the twenty-first century; rather, each of the chapters you are about to read is a partial, particular, or concrete reading attempting to bring out an unexpected (or repressed or obscured) universal dimension in what might even seem marginal and appear to originate from just a (sometimes even only distant) sideways glance at Marx. This book also does not seek to represent an evaluation of the almost countless previous readings presented in the twentieth century and earlier. Our approach is not only partial; it is also decidedly non-encyclopedic. Rather, in each of our respective readings we engage in an attempt to produce something unexpected (in and/ or from Marx), and readers will judge for themselves whether this experiment works and where precisely it may, will, or has failed. Thus, this book might be read as a contribution to an unexpected reunion of Marx(ism). Why an unexpected reunion?

Ernst Bloch (as well as Franz Kafka) once declared a story of Johann Peter Hebel – unexpected reunion – to be "the most beautiful history of the world."[16] This story begins with a young mineworker who was about to get married; one day close to the wedding, he does not return from the mine and has apparently died somewhere

15

therein. When, after fifty years, a part of this mine collapses, the corpse of the young worker comes to light – fully conserved and not aged a day, as it had been lying in a liquid all these years, which kept the body as it was when the mineworker died. At first no one recognizes him, since all his relatives had died in the years since his disappearance, but then an old woman with grey hair and a crutch, his former bride-to-be, comes to see the body and recognizes him immediately. She participates in his burial – "as if it were her wedding day" – and when his body is lowered into the grave, she leaves him saying: "Sleep well for another day or a week or so longer in your cold wedding bed, and don't let time weigh heavy on you! I have only a few things left to do, and I shall join you soon, and soon the day will dawn."

This book is an attempt to create an unexpected reunion with Marx, not to bury him and us once and for all, but to reflect on possible ways of how to reunite emancipatory thinking (again) with his name: since maybe we have only a few things left to do, and we shall join him soon, and "soon the day will dawn" – philosophy's hour has always been the moment when day turns to dusk. So, let us begin doing what needs to be done: reading Marx.

Berlin/Ljubljana/Prishtina

1

Marx Reads Object-Oriented Ontology

The reading of Marx we really need today is not so much a direct reading of his texts as an imagined reading: the anachronistic practice of imagining how Marx would have answered to new theories proposed to replace the supposedly outdated Marxism. The latest in this series is a complex field whose different versions go under the names of object-oriented ontology (OOO), assemblage theory, and new materialism (NM). Although its main target is transcendental humanism, what lurks in the background is clearly the specter of Marxism. In defending Marxism against this latest onslaught, we will proceed via an unexpected detour: our reading of OOO will privilege Graham Harman who, although he may appear to offer its most static and undialectical version, paradoxically brings out some features which enable us to establish a link with Marxist dialectics.[1]

Mechanism, organism, structure, totality, assemblage – one should negotiate a proper position between the two extremes: the assertion of just one category (say, assemblage or totality) as the only appropriate one, with the denunciation of others as false; the simple acceptance of each category as an appropriate description of a particular level of reality (mechanism for inanimate matter, organism for life, etc.). Especially interesting are cases of the dialectical intermingling of categories – for example, does Stephen Jay Gould's thesis on exaptation not imply that organisms are structured like assemblages? Does Hegel's deployment of the rise of Spirit out of Life not imply a "regression" to mechanism at the level of how signs function? (It is this "regression" to mechanism that sustains the passage from organic-expressive Whole characteristic of organisms to differential structure characteristic of symbolic networks.) The crucial point is, then, that the five notions – mechanism, organism, (differential) structure, totality, assemblage – are not at the same level. Totality is not the same as differential structure, but only in the sense that totality is differential structure thought to the end – that is, a differential structure that includes subjectivity and a constitutive antagonism. (Furthermore, mechanism of dead matter is not the same as the signifying mechanism.) Bearing all this in mind, we'll focus on the opposition between assemblage and totality. Let us begin with the basic determinations of assemblage:

1. Assemblages are relational: they are arrangements of different entities linked together to form a new whole. They consist of relations of exteriority, and this exteriority implies certain autonomy of the terms (people, objects, etc.) from the relations between them; the properties of the component parts also cannot explain the relations that constitute a whole.
2. Assemblages are productive: they produce new terri-

torial organizations, new behaviors, new expressions, new actors, and new realities.

3. Assemblages are heterogeneous: there are no a priori limits as to what can be related – humans, animals, things, and ideas – nor is there a dominant entity in an assemblage. As such, assemblages are socio-material, i.e., they eschew the nature-culture divide.

4. Assemblages imply a dynamic of deterritorialization and reterritorialization: they establish territories as they emerge and hold together but also constantly mutate, transform, and break up.

5. Assemblages are desired: desire constantly couples continuous flows and partial objects that are by nature fragmentary and fragmented.

In this vision, the world is conceived as multiple and performative, that is, shaped through practices, as different from a single pre-existing reality. This is why, for Bruno Latour, politics should become material, a Dingpolitik revolving around things and issues of concern, rather than around values and beliefs. Stem cells, mobile phones, genetically modified organisms, pathogens, new infrastructure, and new reproductive technologies bring concerned publics into being that create diverse forms of knowledge about these matters and diverse forms of action – beyond institutions, political interests, or ideologies that delimit the traditional domain of politics. Whether it is called ontological politics, Dingpolitik, or cosmopolitics, this form of politics recognizes the vital role of nonhumans, in concrete situations, co-creating diverse forms of knowledge that need to be acknowledged and incorporated rather than silenced. Particular attention has gone to that most central organization of all for political geographers: the state. Instead of conceiving the state as a unified actor, it should be approached as an assemblage that makes heterogeneous points of order – geographic, ethnic, linguistic, moral, economic, technological particularities – resonate together. As such, the state is an effect rather than the origin of power, and one should focus on reconstructing the socio-material basis of its functioning. The concept of assemblage questions the naturalization of hegemonic assemblages and renders them open to political challenge by exposing their contingency. "By insisting that phenomena do not have to be a particular way just because they are a particular way, assemblage thinking and ANT [actor-network theory] open up avenues for alternative orderings and thus for political action."[2]

The relative autonomy of the elements of an assemblage also enables the radical re-contextualization of a work of art; exemplary here, of course, is the case of Shakespeare's plays, which can be transposed into a contemporary setting and given a different twist without losing their effectiveness. But let us take another more surprising example. Of the three post-WWII big versions of the movie *Quo Vadis* (1951, USA, Melvyn le Roy; 1985, TV miniseries, Italy, Franco Rossi; 2001, Poland, Jerzy Kawalerowicz), the first and the last are exemplary cases of "high quality" religious kitsch, while Rossi's six-hour TV version with Klaus Maria Brandauer as Nero is much more unsettling in its dark mood. In this version, there is so much perverse darkness in the obscene power display of Nero and his court that the final redemption simply doesn't work – the surviving Christians are just left to depart after their lives were effectively ruined and their innocent joy of life destroyed. Rossi demonstrates how a model cinema version should proceed: even the lowest form of Christian propaganda (Henryk Sienkiewicz's unbearably pretentious novel, which got him the Nobel Prize) can be rendered in a way that counteracts its explicit message. Rossi does not introduce a foreign element into the novel – the narrative content is exactly the same; he merely takes the atmosphere of perverse tortures of the early Christians more seriously than the original novel did itself. So, to put it in the terms of ANT, Rossi's version is contained in the novel's diagram, as a virtual option. However, the conclusion that I draw from this example is not exactly the same as the one drawn by Harman. Rossi's version is not contained in the novel In-itself; it was added to the novel's diagram with the new trends in cinema. Furthermore, such a "change" is not the result of some mysterious In-itself of the novel that eludes its actual interactions; if we want to discern how such a different reading is rendered possible by the immanent structure of the novel, we should rather conceive the novel as in itself ontologically open, "unfinished," inconsistent, traversed by antagonisms. I am basically making here the traditional Hegelian point: change doesn't come just from outside. In order for a thing to (be able to) change, its identity already has to be "contradictory," inconsistent, full of immanent tensions, and in this sense ontologically "open." [In-itself? in-itself? in itself? Later on, the hyphenated version is always given with an initial capital letter: In-itself.]

In the domain of politics, it would be interesting to analyze the Trump movement as an assemblage – not as a consistent *sui generis* populist movement, but as a precarious assemblage of heterogeneous elements that enabled it to exert hegemony: populist anti-establishment protest rage, protection of the rich by lower taxes, fundamentalist Christian morality, racist patriotism, etc. These elements in no way belong together; they are heterogeneous and can as easily be combined into a totally different set (for example, anti-establishment protest rage was also exploited by Bernie Sanders; lower taxes for the rich are usually advocated on purely economic grounds by (economic) liberals who despise populism, etc.).

The logic of assemblage is also to be taken into account when we are dealing with big Leftist emancipatory slogans like "the struggle against Islamophobia and the struggle for women's rights are one and the same struggle" – yes, as a goal, but in the mess of actual politics these are two separate struggles that not only run independently of each other but also work against each other: Muslim women's struggle against their oppression; anticolonial struggle, which dismisses women's rights as a Western plot to destroy traditional Muslim communal life, etc.

The concept of assemblage also opens up a path to the key question of the communist reorganization of society: how could one put together in a different way large-scale organizations that regulate water supply, health, security, etc.? We should raise here the question of how the notion of assemblage relates to Ernesto Laclau's notion of the chain of equivalences, which also involves a combination of heterogeneous elements that can be combined with different others (for example, ecology can be anarchic, conservative, capitalist – believing that market regula-tions and taxations are the right measures – communist, state-interventionist . . .). What distinguishes Laclau's "chain of equivalences" is that such a chain does not only assemble heterogeneous elements into an agency, it assembles them as part of the antagonistic struggle of Us against Them, and antagonism is something that traverses each of these elements from within. This is why we should not conceive assemblage as a combination of pre-given elements that strive toward some kind of unification: each element is already traversed by a universality which cuts into it as a universal antagonism/inconsistency, and it is this antagonism that pushes elements to unify, to form assemblages. The desire-for-assemblage is thus proof that a dimension of universality is already at work in all elements in the guise of negativity, of an obstacle that thwarts their self-identity. In other words, elements don't strive for assemblage in order to become part of a larger Whole; they strive for assemblage in order to become themselves, to actualize their identity.

Dialectical Materialism is Immaterialism

Before we deal with this central topic of the relationship between assemblage and antagonism, we should clarify what Harman means by his anti-materialist stance (directed against other currents close to his) or, as he calls it, his "immaterialism." In this short overview, I of course largely ignore the important differences between object-oriented ontology, actor-network theory, and new materialism (these differences are concisely deployed by Harman). The opposition of NM and Harman's own immaterialism is the one between constant change of everything (flux) and intermittent change with stability as a norm – continuity of flow versus fixed identities and definite boundaries; everything is contingent versus not everything is contingent; actions/verbs versus substances/nouns; interactive practice versus autonomous essences; what a thing does versus what a thing is; multiple versus singular; immanence versus transcendence. And between ANT and OOO: the two share a basic ontology, but everything is an actor (ANT) versus action is not a universal property (OOO); reciprocity of action (ANT) versus non-reciprocity (OOO); and symmetry versus asymmetry of relations; etc. Basically, it is the Deleuzean concept of becoming versus a return to stable identities of being – a stance that is today more or less universally accepted. Who dares to deny that stable "essences" and clearly delimitated entities are just temporary "reifications" of some productive flux of becoming? The key difference between Harman's theory and ANT is that, in ANT, assemblage's unity is purely relational, irreducible to its component parts – and, paradoxically, I am here on Harman's side, although, of course, with a twist. The first of Harman's "Fifteen Provisional Rules of OOO Method" is: objects not actors – "things pre-exist their activity rather than being created by it."[3] His main argument for the stable "essential" identity of objects is paradoxically (the possibility of) change: if objects were totally externalized, actualized in their interactions with other objects, all their potentials would have been always already actualized and there would be no space for change.

There are many ways to discern materialism, the materialist position, today. One would be to insist on a minimal link of every universality to a particular species: a universality is never purely abstract, a neutral medium of its species; it always entertains a privileged link to one of its species – Hegel called this "concrete universality." So where should we look for materialism today? Let us turn to quantum physics, the supreme battleline between materialism and idealism. In April 2017, a media report claimed that

> Scientists have discovered a new mechanism in quantum mechanics that challenges existing knowledge about the point at which entangled light particles originate from.
>
> Quantum entanglement is the process where seemingly pairs or groups of counter-intuitive matter instantly affect each other, for example, the measurement of one particle on Earth instantly affecting another particle at the opposite end of the universe. . . .
>
> Researchers from the University of East Anglia (UEA) were researching Spontaneous Parametric Down Conversion (SPDC), which is one of the main ways that pairs of entangled photons are generated, by passing a beam of photons through a crystal to create entangled photon pairs.
>
> It has always been commonly believed that the process works by having one photon goes into the crystal, die, and then two new entangled photons are born in the same location, space and time as the one that died. However, the researchers found that the entangled pair of photons can actually originate from somewhere else in the crystal.
>
> "The place of birth of the two new photons need not be co-located because it's possible to connect them in the vacuum field, which is a standard facet of quantum theory. Throughout our universe, there is a background of residual energy which you can't normally tap – it's an energy associated with light when there are no photons present called vacuum fluctuations," Dr. David Andrews, a professor of chemistry at UEA's School of Chemistry, told IBTimes UK.
>
> "The background is essentially borrowing the energy from the vacuum fluctuations, coupled together where the two

new photons originated. It is the vacuum field that is connecting those two points."[4]

To simplify it to the utmost, the point is that, to account for the process referred to here (entanglement), it is not enough to have particles (photons) moving in empty space – the space in which photons move has to be a vacuum that is not simply empty, but full of vacuum fluctuations in which virtual particles appear and vanish continuously. Even when a photon–photon interaction seems to take place in an empty field, it can only occur through the interaction with the vacuum state of some other field. This, perhaps, provides a minimum of materialism: every interaction of actual particles has to be sustained by the vacuum fluctuations of virtual particles; it cannot take place in an absolute void. The interesting point here is that the situation is the exact opposite of what one would have expected: materialism doesn't mean that every immaterial virtuality has to be sustained by actual material particles, but, on the contrary, that every actual interaction has to be sustained by the virtual background of vacuum fluctuations.

Harman equates "immaterialism" with the notion of substantial objects, objects which exist in-themselves, independently of their relations to other objects – but the notion of substantial objects which exist in-themselves is usually perceived as the basic idea of materialism. In our common sense, "materialism" means that our reality does not consist only of relations or waves or vibrations; there must be a hard "something" that vibrates, relates to other somethings, interacts with them, etc. This is why materialism looked with such suspicion upon quantum physics, which seemed to "dissolve" substantial matter in fields of immaterial waves, as far as interpreting particles as knots/intersections of waves:

> Particles are epiphenomena arising from fields. Thus the Schroedinger field is a space-filling physical field whose value at any spatial point is the probability amplitude for an interaction to occur at that point. The field for an electron *is* the electron; each electron extends over both slits in the 2-slit experiment and spreads over the entire pattern.[5]

And if we find such "disappearance of (substantial) matter" in fields of relations at the lowest level of elementary particles (the now half-abandoned string theory clearly expresses this view), we find it also at the "highest" level of spirituality. Fichte's idealist definition of subject is that it is an entity that fully coincides with its activity: it is immaterial since it "is" only insofar as its act, and it "posits" itself in this acting. More broadly, Hegel differentiates between material and spiritual substances: a spiritual substance has no reality, it is a virtual entity which exists only insofar as it is kept alive through the incessant activity of its real members or agents. For example, communism as a political Cause exists only insofar as there are communists who struggle for it, and it is also materialized in a series of institutions, practices, and material objects (flags, etc.); although the Cause only exists in these material elements and is their effect, it is also in a more fundamental way their cause, what motivates all these individuals and institutions in their activity. And, for a materialist (but also for Hegel and Kierkegaard), God is in this same sense a purely relational entity, something that exists only as the effect of the believers' spiritual and material practices, and at the same time functions as their motivating Cause. This relational status does not mean that such entities are totally (self-)transparent: they have their own impenetrable In-itself, and we can legitimately debate their hidden destructive potentials (recall the legitimate question of how the very original idea of communism already harbors dark potentials, which exploded in Stalinism). The status of this In-itself is very interesting: although the entity in question ("communism") is purely relational, this doesn't mean that we can reduce it to a passive effect of "really existing" people and their material practices: a relational entity also can have its hidden side, its In-itself. It is a stable entity, but an entity in which stability and change coincide: its stability is maintained by incessant change and activity of its agents – if this activity stops, the Cause itself disintegrates.

In a traditional universe, normative structures are presupposed as objective fact, while in modern alienation, they are reduced to expressions of subjective attitudes. The "reconciliation" is achieved when both aspects are perceived in their interaction and mutual dependence: there is no normative substance in itself; normative structures exist only through the constant interaction of individuals engaged in them. However, the necessary result of this interaction is what Jean-Pierre Dupuy calls the "self-transcendence" of a symbolic structure – to be operative, a normative system has to be perceived as autonomous and in this sense "alienated." A somewhat pathetic example: when a group of people fight for communism, they of course know that this idea exists only through their engagement, but they nonetheless relate to it as to a transcendent entity that regulates their lives and for which they may even be ready to sacrifice their lives. One should note here that, for Hegel, alienation is precisely the view that conceives objective normative structures as mere expressions/products of subjective activity, as its "reified" or "alienated" effects. In other words, overcoming alienation is, for Hegel, not the act of dissolving the illusion of autonomy of normative structures, but the act of accepting this "alienation" as necessary. "Spiritual Substance" is Hegel's name for the "big Other," and insofar as the illusion of "big Other" is necessary for the functioning of the symbolic order, one should reject as pseudo-materialist the thought that wants to dismiss this dimension. The big Other is effective, it exerts its efficiency in regulating real social processes, not in spite of its nonexistence but because it doesn't exist – only an inexistent virtual order can do the job. So one should resist the temptation to dismiss every such structure of "self-transcendence" (a system which, although engendered and sustained by the continuous activity of the subjects who participate in it, is (necessarily) perceived by them as a fixed entity which exists independently of their activity) as a case of "self-alienation" or "reification." Is the VOC (United East India Company) analyzed by Harman not also such a virtual entity – virtual in the sense that it exists only in and through the activity of its agents, yet it has an agency of its own? And what about Capital – is it not such a purely relational virtual entity that nonetheless acts as an agent of its self-reproduction?

Dupuy's paramount example is that of the market: although we know that the price of a commodity depends on the interaction of the millions of participants in the market, each individual participant treats the price as an objectively imposed independent value. But is the true principal example not what Lacan calls the "big Other"

– that is, the symbolic order? Although this order has no objective existence independently of the interaction of subjects engaged in it, each subject has to accomplish a minimal "reification" or "alienation," treating the order as an objective entity determining the individuals. Far from indicating a pathological case, this "alienation" is the very measure of normality, that is, of the normativity inscribed into language: in order for us to really obey a norm – say, the norm not to spit in public – it is not enough to say to ourselves "the majority of people do not spit in public"; we have to go one step further and say: "One does not spit in public!" The simple majority of individuals has to be replaced by the minimally "reified" anonymous impersonal "one."

A nice example of the hidden potentials of such an ideal Cause is provided by "human rights": when they first emerged, they were de facto limited to white men of property, but they soon acquired a dynamic of their own and were expanded to women, children, blacks, slaves, etc. This is why Spinoza was fatefully too narrow in his equation of power and right: for Spinoza, justice means that every entity is allowed to freely deploy its inherent power potentials, that is, the amount of justice owed to me equals my power. Spinoza's ultimate thrust is here anti-legalistic: the model of political impotence is, for him, the reference to an abstract law which ignores the concrete differential network and relationship of forces. A "right" is, for Spinoza, always a right to "do," to act upon things according to one's nature, not the (judicial) right to "have," to possess things. It is precisely this equation of power and right that, in the very last page of his *Tractatus Politicus*, Spinoza evokes as the key argument for the "natural" inferiority of women:

[I]f by nature women were equal to men, and were equally distinguished by force of character and ability, in which human power and therefore human right chiefly consist; surely among nations so many and different some would be found, where both sexes rule alike, and others, where men are ruled by women, and so brought up, that they can make less use of their abilities. And since this is nowhere the case, one may assert with perfect propriety that women have not by nature equal right with men.[6]

Here, Harman is right: in Spinoza's view, the potentiality of women to act in a different way, not as inferior to men, disappears, since he reduces women to the actuality of their social relations, where they are (or, rather, were in his time) subordinated to men.

Diagram Traversed by Antagonism

The surplus of identity over the dynamics of interaction does not point toward some stable inner core of the object, but is the surplus of virtual potentiality over reality, the surplus deployed in what Manuel DeLanda calls the diagram of an object. One should thus thoroughly reject the "dynamic" image of reality where every fixed identity is a fixation of its process of becoming, where every delimitation is a temporary fixation of the flux of becoming. Furthermore, "stability" is the stable virtual point of the impossible/real, the antagonism of the barred One, the deadlock that triggers incessant activity. Also, it is important to note that the premise that one acts because of what one is, not vice versa, echoes the Protestant doctrine of grace and predestination, also a "static" view which motivates breathtaking dynamics.

Constanze's aria in the middle of Mozart's opera *The Abduction from the Seraglio* consists of two parts: after the spoken and orchestral interlude, it culminates in "Martern aller Arten" (Act II, Nos. 10 and 11), where it explodes in a dramatic intensity totally out of place in a rococo Singspiel – Mozart here uncannily announces Wagner. From the pre-Wagnerian point of view, this strange conjunction of two arias is doubtlessly a dramatic musical weakness; however, as soon as we measure it from Wagner, this "weakness" can be read as pointing toward truly Wagnerian dramatic intensity. Again, it depends which diagram we ascribe to the aria.

When assemblage theory wants to think of individuals as outside the standard Aristotelian triad of universal/particular/individual, how can it explain the regularity and stability of the characteristics of the individual entities? Something has to be added to perform the role that genera and species play in Aristotelian ontology. These regularities "can be explained by adding a diagram to the assemblage, that is, by conceiving of the space of possibilities associated with its dispositions as being structured by singularities."[7] Instead of the genus of an assemblage, we thus need "the virtual structure of possibility spaces constituting its diagram"; in the case of an animal, "this involves a proper conceptualization of a topological animal that can be folded and stretched into the multitude of different animal species that populate the world,"[8] or, to quote Deleuze and Guattari, a "single abstract Animal for all assemblages that effectuate it":

A unique plane of consistency or composition for the cephalopod and the vertebrate; for the vertebrate to become an Octopus or Cuttlefish, all it would have to do is fold itself in two fast enough to fuse the elements of the halves of its back together, then bring its pelvis up to the nape of its neck and gather its limbs together into one of its extremities.[9]

Such topological transformations "cannot, of course, be performed on adult animals: only the embryos of those animals are flexible enough to endure them."[10] So here, we do not get the abstract universality of Animal, but a matrix of all variations and permutations that is not an atemporal structure (as in Lévi-Strauss), but a diagram of its becoming-individuation, of all possible genetic processes. The diagram of an assemblage is its transcendental dimension, transcendental in Deleuze's sense. At this abstract level (of the distinction between a singularity and its diagram, its transcendental frame), we can define a revolution as a transcendental change where this singularity's virtual background is transformed and what was impossible becomes possible. Nothing had to "really change" in a revolution – to take an example from *Ninotchka*: for a cup of coffee, a revolution is when it changes from a cup of coffee without milk to a cup of coffee without cream. In the same way, in eroticism, new "potentialities" of sexual pleasure are what a good lover brings out in you: s/he sees them in you even though you were unaware of them. They are not a pure In-itself, which was already there before it was discovered; they are an In-itself that is generated through a relationship with the other (lover). The same holds for a good teacher/ leader who "trusts in you" and, in this way, enables you to develop unexpected potentials. It is too simple to say that, before they were discovered, these potentials were already dormant in you as your In-itself. It is here that I cannot agree with Graham Harman: what an object is in itself, beyond its actual relations and interactions with others, is not immanent to it independently of its relations to others; it is, rather, dependent on its relations to others. When a cup of coffee is put in relation to milk, coffee-without-milk becomes a part of its diagram, a "proximate failure" of milk.

This is why Harman is right in emphasizing how failure is the key to identity: what things *are* (in excess over their actions) are their failures registered in their virtual dimension. As Harman puts it in his Rule 4, "an object is better known by its proximate failures than by its successes"; proximate failures are "neighboring failures that were not a foregone conclusion," and they "also give rise to 'ghost' objects that offer fuel for endless counterfactual speculation, not all of it worthless."[11] The identity of an object, its In-itself, resides in its diagram, in virtualities of which only some are actualized. Here, however, a further distinction is to be introduced: in the panoply of failures (or non-actualized potentials) one should distinguish those whose non-actualization is effectively an accidental fact from those, much more interesting, whose non-actualization appears as accidental but is effectively essential to the identity of the object in question – it appears something could have happened, but its actual taking-place would ruin the identity of the object. DeLanda's concept of "diagram" (the matrix of all possible variations of an assemblage object, its virtual echo) should thus be crucially amended: it is not enough to say that some variations are actualized while others remain a possibility. Some variations are essentially non-realized – that is, although they appear as possibilities, they have to remain mere possibilities; if they are accidentally actualized, the entire structure of a diagram

34

disintegrates. They are the point of the impossible-real of a structure, and it is crucial to identify them. Let us take today's capitalism as a global system: its hegemony is sustained by the liberal pragmatic idea that one can solve problems gradually, one by one ("people are dying now in Rwanda, so forget about anti-imperialist struggle, let us just prevent the slaughter"; or, "one has to fight poverty and racism here and now, not waiting for the collapse of the global capitalist order"). John Caputo wrote:

> I would be perfectly happy if the far left politicians in the United States were able to reform the system by providing universal health care, effectively redistributing wealth more equitably with a revised IRS code, effectively restricting campaign financing, enfranchising all voters, treating migrant workers humanely, and effecting a multilateral foreign policy that would integrate American power within the international community, etc., i.e., intervene upon capitalism by means of serious and far-reaching reforms. . . . If after doing all that Badiou and Žižek complained that some Monster called Capital still stalks us, I would be inclined to greet that Monster with a yawn.[12]

The problem here is not Caputo's conclusion: if one can achieve all that within capitalism, why not remain there? The problem is the underlying "utopian" premise that it is possible to achieve all that within the coordinates of present global capitalism. What if the particular malfunctionings of capitalism enumerated by Caputo are not only accidental disturbances but structurally necessary? What if Caputo's dream is a dream of universality (the universal capitalist order) without its symptoms, without the critical points in which its "repressed truth" articulates itself?

Antagonism and Universality

We encounter the same problem when we try to clarify how to relate the universal struggle for emancipation to the plurality of ways of life; nothing should be left to chance, not even the most self-evident general notions. Left liberals view the very notion of "way of life" with suspicion (as long as it doesn't relate to marginal minorities, of course), as if it conceals a proto-fascist poison. Against this suspicion, one should accept the term in its Lacanian version, as something that points beyond all cultural features toward a core of the Real, of *jouissance* – a "way of life" is ultimately the way in which a certain community organizes its *jouissance*. This is why "integration" is such a sensitive issue: when a group is under pressure to "integrate" into a wider community, it often resists out of fear that it will lose its mode of *jouissance*. A way of life does not encompass just rituals of food, music and dance, social life, etc., but also and above all habits, written and unwritten rules, of sexual life (inclusive of rules of mating and marriage) and of social hierarchy (respect for elders, etc.). In India, for example, some postcolonial theorists defend even the caste system as part of a specific way of life that should be defended against the onslaught of global individualism.

To deal with this problem, the preferred vision is that of a united world with multiple particular ways of living, each one of which asserts its difference from others without antagonism, not at the expense of others, but as a positive display of creativity that contributes to the wealth of the entire society. When an ethnic group is prevented from expressing/producing its identity in this creative way because it is under pressure to renounce it and "integrate" into the predominant (usually Western) culture and way of life, it cannot but react, withdrawing into negative difference, a regressive purist fundamentalism that fights the predominant culture, including resorting to violent means. In short, fundamentalist violence is a reaction for which the predominant culture is responsible.

This entire vision of creative differences, of particular identities contributing to a united world, and threatened by the violent pressure on the minorities to "integrate" – in other words, by the false universality of the Western way of life, which imposes itself as a standard for all – is to be rejected in its entirety. The world we live in is one, but it is one because it is traversed (and in that way even held together) by the same antagonism, the one inscribed into the very heart of global capitalism. Universality is not unrelated to particular identities; it is not their neutral container, but an antagonism that emerges from within each of way of life. All emancipatory struggles are over-determined by this antagonism: explicit and unwritten rules of hierarchy, homophobia, male domination, etc., are all key constituents of a way of life in which such struggles occur. Let us take the very sensitive case of China and Tibet. The brutal Chinese colonization of Tibet is a fact, but this fact should not make us blind to what kind of country Tibet was before 1949 and even before 1959 – an extremely harsh feudal and hierarchical society, regulated down to the last detail. In the late 1950s, when the Chinese authorities still more or less tolerated the Tibetan way of life, a villager visited his relatives in a neighboring village without asking his feudal master for permission. When the villager was caught and threatened with severe punishment, he took refuge in a nearby

Chinese military garrison, but when his master learned this, he complained that the Chinese were brutally meddling in the Tibetan way of life – and he was right! So what should the Chinese do? A similar example is that of a traditional Tibetan custom that has undergone a strange transformation over the last half-century:

> During the Cultural Revolution, if an old landowner met emancipated serfs on the road he would stand to the side, at a distance, putting a sleeve over his shoulder, bowing down and sticking out his tongue – a courtesy paid by those of lower status to their superiors – and would only dare to resume his journey after the former serfs had passed by. Now things have changed back: the former serfs stand at the side of the road, bow and stick out their tongues, making way for their old lords. This has been a subtle process, completely voluntary, neither imposed by anyone nor explained.[13]

In short, the ex-serfs somehow detected that with Deng Xiaoping's "reforms," they were once again at the bottom of the social scale. However, much more interesting than the redistribution of social hierarchy signaled by this change is the fact that the same traditional ritual survived such tremendous social transformations. In order to dispel any illusions about Tibetan society, is it not enough to note the distasteful nature of this custom. Over and above the usual stepping aside and bowing – to add insult to injury, as it were – the subordinated individual had to fix his face in an expression of humiliating stupidity (open mouthed with tongue stretched out, eyes turned upwards, etc.) in order to signal with this grotesque grimace his worthless stupidity. The crucial point here is to recognize the violence of this practice, a violence that no consideration of cultural differences and no respect for otherness should ignore. Again, in cases like these, where does respect for the other's way of life reach its limit? True, we should not intervene from outside, imposing our standards, but is it not the duty of every fighter for emancipation to unconditionally support those in the other culture who, from within, resist such oppressive customs.

Anticolonialists, as a rule, emphasize how the colonizers try to impose universally their own culture and thereby undermine the indigenous way of life. But what about the opposite strategy, which resides in strengthening local traditions in order to make colonial domination more efficient? No wonder the British colonial administration of India elevated *The Laws of Manu* – a detailed justification and manual of the caste system – into the privileged text to be used as a reference for establishing the legal code that would render possible the most efficient domination of India. Up to a point, one can even say that *The Laws of Manu* only became *the* book of the Hindu tradition retroactively. And, in a more subtle way, the Israeli authorities are doing the same on the West Bank: they silently tolerate (or at least do not investigate seriously) "honor killings," being well aware that the true threat to them are not devout Muslim traditionalists, but modern Palestinians. This is the lesson that not only refugees, but all members of traditional communities, should learn: the way to strike back at cultural neocolonialism is not to resist it on behalf of the traditional culture but to reinvent a more radical modernity – something Malcolm X was well aware of.

It is this unreadiness to accept the primary role of universality which saps the bulk of postcolonial studies. Ramesh Srinivasan's book, *Whose Global Village?*[14]

is representative of the efforts to "decolonize" digital technology, and one hallmark of his work is the strange (literally uncanny) recourse to the term "ontology" to designate its exact opposite, a radical historicization of every ontology – that is, the fact that every ontology (view of reality) is an effect of historically specific semiotic practices. Why this word? For Srinivasan, digital technology is not just a neutral-universal technological frame of the exchange between cultures, since it privileges a certain (Western modern) culture, so that even benevolent efforts to extend computer literacy and include everyone into the digital "global village" secretly prolong colonization, imposing integration of the subaltern into Western modernity and thus oppressing their cultural specificity. What Srinivasan means by "ontology" is the fact that our knowledge of reality never just mirrors reality, but is always grounded in a specific community and its cultural practices: "I work with the concept of ontology to consider how knowledge is articulated culturally" (p. 34). Or, quoting John Law, "objects, entities, actors, processes – all are semiotic effects" (p. 36). Srinivasan mentions briefly that communities themselves are "multifaceted and diverse," but instead of developing this point into the notion of antagonisms that traverse every community, he waters it down into global relativization and partiality of every view:

> Recognizing that a fluid ontology is partial. Simply because an ontology is generated by a group of community members does not mean that their choices completely reflect others in the community whom they may claim to represent, or even represent themselves fully. All communities are diverse and multifaceted. Instead of this being an obstacle, this com-

plexity can be embraced by the humble recognition that no ontology is totalizing. (p. 137)

This brings us to the crux of the problem, to Srinivasan's use of the term "ontology": the basic ontological unity of his vision of reality comprises communities which, through their life-practices, form their own vision of reality. They are the starting point, and "conversations that surpass the bounds of community" come second, so that when we practice them we should always be careful to respect the authentic voice of the particular community. Therein resides the trap of the popular notion of the "global village": it imposes on non-Western communities assumptions that are not theirs; that is, it practices cultural colonialism.

> While it is important to learn about other people, cultures, and communities on their terms, we must respect the power and importance of local, cultural, indigenous, and community-based creative uses of technology. Conversations that surpass the bounds of community can and should emerge but only when the voices of their participants are truly respected. From this perspective, the "global village" is the problem rather than the solution. We must reject assumptions about technology and culture that are dictated by Western concepts of cosmopolitanism. (p. 209)

This is why Srinivasan criticizes Ethan Zuckerman, who "is correct to say that many of today's challenges, such as climate change, require global conversation and cross-cultural awareness. But not all challenges are global and indeed thinking globally about people's traditions, knowledges, struggles, and identities may unintentionally exclude them from positions of control and power"

(p. 213) So, again, the global view is strictly secondary; what comes first is the multiplicity of local communities with their particular "ontologies." And even modern science in its global reach is historically relativized as just one among a number of practices of knowledge with no right to be privileged – Srinivasan approvingly quotes Boaventura de Sousa Santos, who claims that "the epistemological privilege granted to modern science from the seventeenth century onwards, which made possible the technological revolutions that consolidated Western supremacy, was also instrumental in suppressing other non-scientific forms and knowledges. . . . It is now time to build a more democratic and just society and . . . decolonize knowledge and power" (p. 224).

It would be easy to show that such "fluid ontology" of the multiplicity of cultures is rounded in a typically Western postmodern view based on the historicization of all knowledge, a view that has nothing to do with actual premodern societies. But much more important is the link between Srinivasan's disavowal of universality (the ontological primacy of particular cultures/communities) and his ignoring of the inner antagonisms constitutive of particular communities: they are two sides of the same misrecognition, since universality is not a neutral frame elevated above particular cultures, but is inscribed into them, at work in them, in the guise of their inner antagonisms, inconsistencies, and disruptive negativities. Every particular way of life is a politico-ideological formation whose task is to obfuscate an underlying antagonism, a particular way of coping with this antagonism, and this antagonism traverses the entire social space. Apart from some tribes in the Amazon jungle who have not yet established contact with modern societies, all communities today are part of global civilization in the sense that their very autonomy has to be accounted for in terms of global capitalism. Let us take the case of native American tribes' attempts to resuscitate their ancient way of life. This way of life was derailed and thwarted by their contact with modern civilization and by the devastating effects of this contact, which left tribes totally disoriented, deprived of a stable communal framework. Their attempts to regain some stability by regaining the core of their traditional way of life depend, as a rule, on their success in finding a niche in the global market economy – many tribes wisely spend the income earned from casinos and mining rights on this resuscitation.

Totality, Antagonism, Individuation

Our main result is thus that what distinguishes totality from assemblage is not some higher organic unity of the assembled elements, but the antagonism that cuts across every assemblage. Totality is not a seamless Whole (without stitches holding different pieces together, functioning without interruptions or difficulties); it is by definition stitched or (to use the Lacanian technical term) sutured. And, for Lacan, the point of suture, the point at which the lack that defines a structure is reflexively inscribed into it, is also the point of the subjectivization of structure: the presence of a subject means that the structure (or totality) in question is traversed by an antagonism, inconsistency, etc. We should go further here: it is not just that totality is split, traversed by antagonism; antagonism is what holds a totality together. What "totalizes" an assemblage of elements is not an all-encompassing universality, but the fact that they are all traversed by the same antagonism. To get this point, we should recognize that totality is not a Whole, but a Whole plus its surpluses that distort it. The passage from the distortion of a notion to a distortion constitutive of this notion is what is enacted in the Hegelian notion of totality: "totality" is not an ideal of an organic Whole, but a critical notion – to "locate a phenomenon in its totality" does not mean seeing the hidden harmony of the Whole, but includes in a system all its distortions ("symptoms," antagonisms, inconsistencies) as its integral parts. In other words, the Hegelian totality is, by definition, "self-contradictory," antagonistic, inconsistent: the "Whole" which is the "True" (Hegel: "*das Ganze ist das Wahre*") is the Whole plus its symptoms, unintended consequences that betray its untruth. For Marx, the "totality" of capitalism includes crises as its integral moment; for Freud, the "totality" of a human subject includes pathological symptoms as indicators of what is "repressed" in the official image of the subject. The underlying premise is that the Whole is never truly whole: every notion of the Whole leaves something out, and the dialectical effort is precisely the effort to include this excess, to account for it. Symptoms are never just secondary failures or distortions of the basically sound system – they are indicators that there is something "rotten" (antagonistic, inconsistent) in the very heart of the system. This is why all the anti-Hegelian rhetoric which insists that Hegel's totality misses the details that stick out and ruin its balance misses the point: the space of the Hegelian totality *is* the very space of the interaction between the ("abstract") Whole and the details that elude its grasp, although they are generated by it. Or, to shift brutally to a concrete case – if you want to talk about global capitalism, you have to include Congo, a country in disarray, with thousands of drugged child-warriors, who are nevertheless, as such, fully integrated into the global system.

This notion of antagonism allows us to put a different spin on a perspicuous saying about the 1960s that is quoted by Harman: "You have to remember that the 1960s really happened in the 1970s." Harman comments: "an object somehow exists 'even more' in the stage following its initial heyday. The marijuana smoking, free love, and internal violence of the dramatic American 1960s were in some ways even better exemplified by the campy and tasteless 1970s."[15] If, however, we take a closer look at the passage from the 1960s to the 1970s, we can easily see the key difference: in the 1960s, the spirit of permissiveness, sexual liberation, counter-culture, and drugs was part of a utopian political protest movement, while, in the 1970s, this spirit was deprived of its political content and fully integrated into the hegemonic culture and ideology. Consequently, "even more" (which means: integration into the hegemonic ideology) was paid for by "much less" (depoliticization), and although we should definitely question the limitation of the spirit of the 1960s that rendered this integration so easy, repression of the political dimension remains a key feature of the popular culture of the 1970s. And does something similar not hold for the Renaissance? It effectively happened back in the fourteenth century with the rise of free states like Florence, where artisans and local democracy were flourishing. But the Renaissance as we know it took place in the late fifteenth and sixteenth centuries, when local princes (Medici, Sforza) squashed local democracy and took over city-states. They supported big artistic geniuses, which gave the Renaissance its name, but the popular democratic impetus was gone. In both cases (the 1960s and the Renaissance), we can see how a thing becomes "even more what it is" through the obfuscation of its constitutive antagonism, that is, through its integration into the hegemonic ideological space.

Antagonism is also what characterizes the ANT notion of individuation, "a relation conceived as a pure or absolute between, a between understood as fully independent of or external to its terms – and thus a between that can just as well be described as 'between' nothing at all."[16] The status of this "absolute between" is that of a pure antagonism. Its structure was deployed by Lacan apropos of sexual difference, which, as a difference, precedes the two terms between which it is the difference. The point of Lacan's "formulae of sexuation" is that both masculine and feminine positions are ways of avoiding the deadlock of the difference as such. This is why Lacan's claim that sexual difference is "real-impossible" is strictly synonymous with his claim that there is no sexual relationship. Sexual difference is, for Lacan, not a firm set of "static" symbolic oppositions and inclusions or exclusions (heterosexual normativity that relegates homosexuality and other "perversions" to some secondary role), but the name of a deadlock, of a trauma, of an open question, of something that resists every attempt at its symbolization. Every translation of sexual difference into a set of symbolic opposition(s) is doomed to fail, and it is this very "impossibility" that opens up the terrain of the hegemonic struggle for what "sexual difference" will mean.

The Inhuman View

Now we can approach the key ontological question: assemblage theory advocates a flat ontology whereby human subjects are reduced to just one among the multiple and heterogeneous actants (to use Latour's term), so how can we accept the subversive edge of this "inhuman view" without regressing into naive realism? Let us take as our starting point Ramon Zurcher's *The Strange Little Cat*, the first true assemblage film in which humans are portrayed as actants among other actants:

> As the family gathers – sons, daughters, their significant others, a sick grandmother, a couple of uncles – they chat with one another, crowding through the kitchen. . . . The monologues continue, and people stroll in and out of the kitchen, down the dark hallway, and back, and the apartment begins to take on a life of its own. Objects start to rebel against the functions they were meant for. Buttons fall off of people's shirts. Drinks spill. The radiator has a weird echo. The washing machine is broken. A glass bottle spins on the stove. A ball flies in through the kitchen window, thrown from the courtyard below, an alarming moment when the bell jar of the family dynamic is shattered by an interloper. At the family dinner later in the film, one of the fat sausages on the table squirts grease wildly when someone cuts into it, causing hilarity.[17]

This "refusal of objects to behave appropriately and do what they were meant to do" indicates that they are also actants in their own right, and that humans are just one among other actants. The question then is: since there are many actants in the film, who is the subject – the mother or the cat? We could say that the mother is the pure subject (she mostly just stares at events and objects without any relevant activity), while the cat is moving around, mediating between other actants, triggering events. The mother and the cat thus stand for the pairing of "$" (the "barred" subject) and "a" (the object cause of desire), and the key scene of the film depicts a weird confrontation of the two: the mother stands near the kitchen sink, her foot, which is raised just above the cat lying on the floor as if tempted to crush it, resting frozen in mid-air. (This scene echoes an accident in the movie theater reported by the mother, which also brings out the immobility of the mother's foot: sitting on her chair, she felt her neighbor, an unknown man, put his shoe on her and leave it there, pressing with his leg on her foot, which she is unable to remove.) And the cat? Toward the film's end, the grandmother dozes off (dies?) in a big chair, and the shot of her is followed by an unexpected and close-up of the cat's head, a shot which, in an uncanny way, subjectivizes the cat. The cat is rendered as somehow linked to the grandmother's death even if not directly responsible for it – is the cat the angel of death? No wonder Zurcher "has described the film as 'a horror movie without any horror,' though it is also a comedy without any actual jokes."[18] We have to take these formulas literally, in the Kantian sense (Kant defines beauty as purposeless purposiveness): pure formal horror which, as such, coincides with comedy.

We can see now in what resides the truly subversive potential of the notion of assemblage: it comes forth when we apply it to describe a constellation that also comprises humans, but from an "inhuman" standpoint, so that humans appear in it as just one among the actants. Recall Jane Bennet's description of how actants interact at a polluted trash site: how not only humans but also the rotting trash, worms, insects, abandoned machines, chemical poisons, and so on each play their (never purely passive) role.[19] There is an authentic theoretical and ethico-political insight in such an approach. When new materialists oppose the reduction of matter to a passive mixture of mechanic parts, they are, of course, not asserting old-fashioned direct teleology, but an aleatoric dynamics immanent to matter: "emerging properties" arise out of non-predictable encounters between multiple kinds of actants, the agency for any particular act is distributed across a variety of kinds of bodies.[20] Agency thereby becomes a social phenomenon, where the limits of sociality are expanded to include all material bodies participating in the relevant assemblage. For example, an ecological public is a group of bodies, some human, most not, that are subjected to harm, defined as a diminished capacity for action. The ethical implication of such a stance is that we should recognize our entanglement within larger assemblages: we should become more sensitive to the demands of these publics and the reformulated sense of self-interest calls upon us to respond to their plight. Materiality, usually conceived as inert substance, should be rethought as a plethora of things that form assemblages of human and nonhuman actors (actants) – humans are but one force in a potentially unbounded network of forces.

One should not be afraid to take this approach to its extreme. Think about Auschwitz as an assemblage – Nazi executioners were involved as its agents, but so too were Jews, the complex network of trains, gas ovens, the logistics of feeding the prisoners, of separating and distributing clothes, golden teeth, hair, ashes, etc. The point of this reading of Auschwitz as an assemblage is not to play vulgar bad taste games, but to bring out the truly subversive character of the assemblage approach, which amounts to looking at Auschwitz with inhuman eyes, or, as Deleuze would have put it, to practice apropos Auschwitz "a perception as it was before men (or after) . . . released from their human coordinates";[21] one should be strong enough to sustain the vision of Auschwitz as part of the "iridescent chaos of a world before man."[22] The standard realist approach aims at describing the world, reality, the way it exists out there, independently of us, observing subjects. But we, subjects, are ourselves part of the world, so the consequent realism should include us in the reality we are describing, so that our realist approach should include describing ourselves "from the outside," independently of ourselves, as if we are observing ourselves through inhuman eyes. What this inclusion of ourselves amounts to is not naive realism, but something much more uncanny, a radical shift in the subjective attitude by means of which we become strangers to ourselves.

There is thus a double paradox at work here. First, such an "inhuman" standpoint from which humans appear just as an agent among others already implies a pure (Cartesian) subject, the only one able to occupy this position. The second paradox (or, rather, question) is: when we view a situation "from outside," can we perceive a subject in it? Is there a subject for an outside view, or from outside do we see only "dead objectivity"? More radically, is a subject (or even life) not always a presupposition, a hypo-thesis? We see something, we impute subjectivity to it, but we cannot ever be sure if subjectivity is really there – what if it is a machine just performing subjectivity? And here we should go one step further: subjectivity *is* in a sense its own performance, something that appears to itself while its "material base" is just a neuronal-biological apparatus.

Although Deleuze here resorts openly to Kant's language, talking about the direct access to "things (the way they are) in themselves," his point is precisely that one should subtract the opposition between phenomena and things-in-themselves, between the phenomenal and the noumenal level, from its Kantian functioning, where noumena are transcendent things that forever elude our grasp. What Deleuze refers to as "things in themselves" is, in a way, even more phenomenal than our shared phenomenal reality: it is the impossible phenomenon, the phenomenon that is excluded from our symbolically constituted reality. The gap that separates us from noumena is thus primarily not epistemological, but practico-ethical and libidinal: there is no "true reality" behind or beneath phenomena; noumena are phenomenal things that are "too strong," too intens(iv)e, for our perceptual apparatus attuned to constituted reality. Epistemological failure is a secondary effect of libidinal terror; that is, the underlying logic is a reversal of Kant's "You can, because you must!": "You cannot (know noumena), because you must not!" Imagine someone being forced to witness a terrifying torture. In a way, the monstrosity of what he saw would make this an experience of the noumenal impossible-real that would shatter the coordinates of our common reality. (The same holds for witnessing an intense sexual activity.) In this sense, if we were to discover films shot in a concentration camp among Muslims, showing scenes from their daily life, how they are systematically mistreated and deprived of all dignity, we would have "seen too much," we would have entered a forbidden territory of what should have remained unseen. (One can well understand Claude Lanzmann who said that if he were to stumble upon such a film, he would destroy it immediately.) This is also what makes it so unbearable to witness the last moments of people who know they are shortly going to die and are in this sense already living-dead. Again, imagine discovering, among the ruins of the Twin Towers, a video camera which miraculously survived the crash intact and is full of shots of what went on among the plane passengers in the minutes before it crashed into one of the towers. In all these cases, it is the case that, effectively, we would have seen things as they are "in themselves," outside human coordinates, beyond our human reality — we would have seen the world with inhuman eyes. (Maybe the US authorities do possess such shots and, for understandable reasons, are keeping them secret.) The lesson here is profoundly Hegelian: the difference between the phenomenal and the noumenal has to be reflected/transposed back into the phenomenal, as does the split between the "gentrified" normal phenomenon and the "impossible" phenomenon.

At the end of Act I of Wagner's *Die Walküre* (in the Chéreau/Boulez staging), following their passionate love duet, Siegmund and Sieglinde lie in an embrace, as if beginning to make love, and at that very moment the curtain closes. In the recording that I have, due to a sudden air movement, the curtain parts again for a split second, rendering the scene visible, and, at this moment, I found myself tempted to check whether the singers were just faking: were they already getting up, straightening their clothes? I was surprised to see that they were still lying in an embrace – was I not able, in this split second, to see the situation as it was "in itself," that is, to observe it with inhuman eyes? Such situations occur also in real life, when I get a sudden glimpse into how things are "behind the curtain" of ordinary reality (in our ordinary life we also play a role – we play ourselves – we are not directly what we are). "In-itself" is not simply the way things are independently of us, it is the immanent point of impossibility of the way things appear to us.

The common notion of a "subjective view" is that of the partial distortion of the objective state of things: our subjective approach distorts the balance of how things really are and privileges one element over all others, allowing it to project its "specific color" over them. In the classic Marxist move, we have to accept that pure abstract universality is impossible to reach – every universality we are dealing with is already overdetermined by some particular content that is privileged with regard to all other particular content, a particular content, which – as Marx would have put it – provides the specific color of the universality in question. There is an irreducible "umbilical cord" on account of which every a priori universality remains attached to (colored, "overdetermined" by) the a posteriori particular content. To put it somewhat bluntly: yes, the universal notional form imposes necessity upon the multitude of its contingent content, but it does it in a way that itself remains marked by an irreducible stain of contingency – or, as Derrida would have put it, the frame itself is always also part of the enframed content. The logic here is that of the Hegelian "oppositional determination [*gegensätzliche Bestimmung*]," in which the universal genus encounters itself among its particular contingent species. Here is Marx's classic example: among the species of production, there is always one that gives the specific color on the universality of production within a given mode of production. In feudal societies, artisanal production itself is structured like another domain of agriculture, while, in capitalism, agriculture itself is "industrialized," that is, it becomes one of the domains of industrial production.

The crucial point here is to see the link between this structure of oppositional determination and subjectivity. Lacan's definition of the signifier is that which "represents the subject for another signifier": not all the signifiers are on the same level – since no structure is complete, since there is, in a structure, always a lack, this lack is filled in, sustained even, re-marked, by a "reflexive" signifier that is the signifier of the lack of the signifier. Identifying the subject with the lack, we can thus say that the reflexive signifier of the lack represents the subject for the other signifiers. If this sounds abstract, recall numerous examples from the history of science, from the phlogiston theory (a pseudo-concept that just betrayed the scientist's ignorance of how light effectively travels) to Marx's "Asiatic mode of production" (which is a kind of negative container: the only true content of this concept is "all the modes of production which do not fit Marx's standard categorization of the modes of production"). Jacques-Alain Miller generates the notion of subject without any reference to the imaginary level: this "subject of the signifier" involves no lived experience, consciousness, or any other predicates we usually associate with subjectivity. The basic operation of suture is thus that o is counted as one: the absence of a determination is counted as a positive determination of its own, as in Jorge Luis Borges's famous classification of dogs, which includes, as a species, all the dogs not included in the previous species, that is, the "part of no-part" of the genus dogs.

We can see now how the usual notion of the "subjective limitation of a perspective" (we always perceive reality from a subjective standpoint, which distorts it) is grounded in the structure of reflexivity through which a structure is subjectivized: not only does a subject perceive reality from its distorted/partial "subjective" standpoint, but the subject only emerges if a structure is itself "distorted" through the privilege of a hegemonic particular element which confers a specific color of universality. But is not the way we described this hegemonic element ambiguous? First, we presented it as the privileged particular element that "colors" its universality (in capitalism, all domains of production appear as species of industrial production); then, we presented it as the "empty" element, which, within a structure, holds the place of what is excluded from it, of its externality (again, in Marxism, the "Asiatic mode of production" de facto holds the place, within the universal series of the modes of production, of what doesn't fit Marx's notion of the mode of production). The balance between universality and its species is thus distributed in two opposite directions: the exceptional element is the particular element that hegemonizes the universality and, simultaneously, the element that represents within the series the external dimension which eludes its universality. The Hegelian-Marxist hypothesis here is that a universality comes to exist as such, in contrast to its particular species, in the guise of its "oppositional determination." To quote Marx's famous example, royalism as such, in contrast to its particular species, exists as republicanism; or, the human species as such, in contrast to its particular groups, exists in the guise of the proletariat, of those who have no specific place within the social body. How are these two exceptions related? The hegemonic element

– industrial production as the "specific color" of every production in capitalism – is obviously not the same as the negation of universality in the guise of which universality as such comes to exist in contrast to its species. One can even say that the relationship between these two universalities provides the minimal form of social antagonism (neglected by Laclau in his elaboration of the concept of antagonism): antagonism is ultimately that which exists between the particular element that hegemonizes universality and the element that, within this universality, stands for what is excluded from it. And it is easy to see the link between the two: in a universality (say, of bourgeois society) there is no place for one of the elements to be excluded from its universal dimension, precisely because this universal dimension is secretly particularized, distorted by the hegemonic predominance of one of its elements. Today, for example, when even individuals who possess nothing or half-starving precarious workers are defined as self-entrepreneurs, so that entrepreneurship is the particular feature that defines everyone engaged in work, the antagonism is still between entrepreneurs and proletarians.

This shift can also be determined as the shift from S_1 (master signifier) to S (barred a), the signifier of the lack/inconsistency of the big Other. The two are in some sense the same, since the auratic presence of the master signifier fills in what is lacking in the big Other; it obfuscates the inconsistency of the symbolic order, and the passage from S_1 to S is ultimately just a shift in perspective which renders palpable this obfuscating function of the master signifier. Here, *objet a* enters: in the master signifier, *objet a* is united with the signifying function, it is the mysterious *je ne sais quoi* which confers on the master signifier its aura, while S1 changes into S when *objet a* is subtracted from the signifying space – that is, when S1 and *objet a* are separated. Through this separation, S1 appears in all its impotence and misery, merely making up for what is lacking.

The Phenomenal In-Itself

The link between subject and antagonism also enables us to approach in a new way the old question: how can we move beyond appearances and reach the In-itself? It is not another world beyond phenomena – things "in themselves" are close to how they appear or how we see/ construct them in sciences; there is no big mystery here. The surplus of the In-itself over the phenomenal reality is ourselves, the gap of subjectivity. What this means, with regard to the gap that separates the transcendental (tran- scendentally constituted reality) from the transcendent In-itself, is that the more we try to isolate reality as it is in itself, independently of the way we relate to it, the more this In-itself falls back into the domain of the transcen- dentally constituted. In short, we go round in circles here, every figure of the In-itself always already caught up in the transcendental circle. But this circle can be broken – the In-itself is not "out there." It is discernible in the very cuts that separate different spheres of the tran- scendentally constituted reality; it is what makes every figuration of "external reality" inconsistent, thwarted, non-all – and these cuts are the sites of the intervention of subjectivity into reality. OOO claims that a subject is an object among objects. But our horizon is transcenden- tally constrained to our subjectivity not because subject is privileged as object, but because it *is* our standpoint.

So how can we break out of it? Not through abstracting from our subjectivity and trying to isolate the way things are in themselves, independently of us – every such attempt fails, since the reality we reach in this way is, as Lacan pointed out, always based on a fantasy that covers up the cut of the Real. We reach the Real only when we reflect on how we fit into the reality of objects around us. This reality is flat, but inconsistent, intercepted by cuts, and these cuts in reality are sites of the inscription of subject. To put it in even more precisely, the vision of "democracy of objects" where all objects occupy the same ontological standing, or the "inhuman" view of an assemblage deployed by Jane Bennet, are only possible from the standpoint of an (empty) subject. Insofar as a subject remains one among the objects, I can only view reality from its particular standpoint; its vision is twisted by the particular coordinates of its specific situation and its interests. It is only the violent abstraction from our particularity that defines a subject which enables us to adopt the view on reality in which humans are one among objects.

This shift in the relationship to the In-itself can be rendered in terms of the shift from the masculine to the feminine position (in the sense of Lacan's formulas of sexuation). The Kantian approach remains masculine: the In-itself is the exception to the universal (transcendental) laws that regulate our phenomenal reality, and we can then engage in the epistemological game of how to erase our distorting lenses and grasp the way things are out there independently of us. For Kant, the In-itself remains beyond our reach; for Locke, properties of a thing that we can perceive only with one sense are subjective, while properties that we can perceive with more than one sense (like shape, which we can see and touch) are properties of the thing in itself; for much of modern science, the In-itself of reality can only be grasped through mathematic formalization. From the Hegelian "feminine" position, the field of phenomena is non-all. It has no exception, there is no In-itself outside, but this field is at the same time inconsistent, cut through by antagonisms. So there is nothing that is not in some way subjectively distorted, but we can discern the In-itself through the very cuts and inconsistencies in the fields of phenomena. In other words, there is a point of impossibility, of an In-itself, in every field of phenomena, but this point – the "stain in the picture" – is not a sign of transcendence that escapes the subject, but the actual stand-in for the subject itself, the inscription of subject into the picture.

So how does the subject enter the game? Here is the first stanza of "Casta Diva" from Bellini's *Norma*: "Casta Diva, che inargenti / Queste sacre antiche piante, / A noi volgi il bel sembiante / Senza nube e senza vel . . ." ("O chaste Goddess, whose silver covers / These sacred ancient plants, / Turn toward us a beautiful semblance / Cloudless and unveiled . . ."). Performed in a night ceremony in the middle of a sacred forest, the incantation addresses Moon, not Sun – that's why the Goddess is chaste, not primarily in the sense of purity but more in the sense of sterility: even when we see it unveiled, without clouds, the light of the Moon is not fertile, it is a mere semblance (although a beautiful one), a pale silver echo of the golden light of the Sun, like the Deleuzean flow of Sense which is a pale effect of bodily causality. And this is the status of subject in Lacan. As Deleuze would have put it, subject is not a mega-substance or a mega-actant, but a sterile surface, basically impotent. $ is an actor that exists only in acting, not in substance. Of course, it has to have some material (neuronal, bodily) base, but "that's not it" – we all know the researcher's surprise: "How can that – the dead meat of our brain – be it (our thought)?" The "Self" stands for the way a human organism experiences itself, appears to itself, and there is *no one* behind the veil of self-appearance, no substantial reality.

> The illusion is irresistible. Behind every face there is a self. We see the signal of consciousness in a gleaming eye and imagine some ethereal space beneath the vault of the skull, lit by shifting patterns of feeling and thought, charged with intention. An essence. But what do we find in that space behind the face, when we look? The brute fact is there is nothing but material substance: flesh and blood and bone and brain. . . . You look down into an open head, watching the brain pulsate, watching the surgeon tug and probe, and you understand with absolute conviction that there is nothing more to it. There's no one there.[23]

How is such an entity, which functions as the appearance of nothing to itself, possible? The answer is clear: such a nonsubstantial entity has to be purely relational, with no positive support of its own. What happens in the passage from substance to subject is thus a kind of reflective reversal: we pass from the secret core of an object inaccessible to other objects to inaccessibility as such — $ is nothing but its own inaccessibility, its own failure to be substance. Therein resides Lacan's achievement: the standard psychoanalytic theory conceives the Unconscious as a psychic substance of subjectivity (the notorious hidden part of the iceberg) – all the depth of desires, fantasies, traumas, etc. – while Lacan desubstantializes the Unconscious (for him, the Cartesian cogito is the Freudian subject), thereby bringing psychoanalysis to the level of modern subjectivity. (It is here that we should bear in mind the difference between the Freudian Unconscious and the "unconscious" neurological brain processes: the latter do form the subject's natural "substance," that is, subject only exists insofar as it is sustained by its biological substance. However, this substance is not subject.)

Subject is not somehow more actant than objects, a mega-actant actively positing all the world of fundamentally passive objects, so that against this hubris one should assert the active role of all objects. At its most fundamental, subject is a certain gesture of passivization, of not-doing, of withdrawal, of passive experience. Subject is, in Lacan's words, "ce qui du réel pâtit du signifiant" ("that which in the Real suffers from the signifier"); its activity is a reaction to this basic feature. So it is not that OOO takes subjectivity into account, merely reducing it to a property or quality of one among other objects. What OOO describes as subject simply does not meet the criteria of the subject – there is no place for the subject in OOO.[24]

2

Marx in the Cave

"Beginning is . . . exiting." (H. Blumenberg)[1]
". . . every eye has a camera obscura . . ." (S. Kofman)[2]

Caving[3]

The history of philosophy, as a famous saying goes, is nothing but footnotes to Plato – struggling with his paradoxes and claims, repeating his questions, attempting to turn against his thought or even moving away from it once and for all. Might one not also claim: the history of critical and emancipatory thought (or philosophy) consists of nothing but footnotes to Plato's cave allegory? Although the reader might be accustomed to the first claim despite or because of its apparent generality, the latter does seem exaggerated. Why should emancipatory thought be a (un)willing adherent to this "striking and brilliant . . . kind of myth"[4]?

The cave allegory presents a pre-enlightenment enlightenment critique of mythical thinking and action. It thereby directly addresses emancipation. But Socrates suggests that one must therefore mythologize the myth ("*en mythò mythologountes*"):[5] to counter one's mythical embeddedness, a "new type of a 'true, untrue' story"[6] is needed, a myth of second degree, an emancipatory fiction. Emancipation has the structure of a fiction.[7] And Plato's fiction addresses it in specific terms, namely of emancipatory anthropogenesis. It formulates in an original manner the theme of emancipation as a real becoming human of the human being, a theme that will be repeated in multiple different ways and versions by many (and not only humanist) thinkers of emancipation. Famously, in Plato, this becoming is linked to exiting the objective (spatial) conditions that inhibit it in the first place. Men in the cave "live, from their earliest childhood, with their legs and necks in chains, so that they have to stay where they are, looking only ahead of them, prevented by the chains from turning their heads."[8] Their gaze is constrained so that they stare in one direction only. This state is thereby also one wherein a fundamental disorientation is produced, as it prevents the very concept of orientation to be formed. The allegory critically deals with this disorientation that prevents emancipation, or the very emergence of a desire for it – since "the shadow-world does . . . not only affect, but infects the inner world"; it "mortifies [the prisoners'] will of liberation."[9]

For those living in the shadows, they appear to be an entirely natural thing[10] and it is hard, if not impossible, to identify them for what they are or to desire something else. It becomes almost impossible to conceive of a strong kind of difference.

In this cavelike dwelling [the prisoners] feel that they are "in the world" and "at home" and here they find what they can rely on . . . in no way do they recognize this prison for what it is . . . They are incapable of even suspecting the possibility that what they take for the real might have the consistency of mere shadows.[11]

The cave prisoners are "not speechless" – they still live in a symbolic universe – but they are fundamentally "without concept"[12] – of what and where they are. Plato's scenario links the adherence to shadows to a prehuman state. Since the disorienting effect – that is not even experienced as disorienting, which is what makes it into what it is – brings it about that the cave inhabitants are "solely determined by the ontology of the world in which they live."[13] In the cave, there is a (human) life that does not live properly. One can thus identify a Platonic cave-allegorical heritage in all projects that try to critically account for and combat such disorienting operations (of naturalization) that prevent human freedom from being realized. The critique of ideology is one of its most prominent names, and emancipatory thought repeatedly sought to break with such (a regionalizing) ontology. This holds independently from how it was brought about; it may be the manifestation of a "self-imposed immaturity" (Kant), or the product of a society wherein there is "a secret identity of commodity form and thought form,"[14] or it may spring from "forms that are always already presupposed."[15] What is at stake in emancipatory thought is almost always an overcoming of a mythical kind of thought and practice – combatting the myth(s) of the (unquestionably) given.

One can, for example, identify an allusion to Plato's cave allegory in Rousseau's famous thesis that "man is born free, and everywhere he is in chains,"[16] or even read the famous criticisms of the "society of spectacle" (Debord) that infects even the very ways in which we think, move, and speak[17] as reappraisals of the Platonic motive. Yet, unchaining man – from whatever chains, real or metaphorical – is an intricate task under certain conditions, and especially if "the social being in which we live exists in a way that it exudes deceptions and nobody, not even a Marxist [!], can withdraw from their influence."[18] The hypothesis I will examine is the following one: what if modern – that is, capitalist – society, in a sense to be specified, resembles a version of Plato's cave? And what if Marx can be read "experimentally," yet consistently, in this vein?[19]

To begin with, what precisely is the cave? What if there is not only a cultural but, even, a natural cave-state of man that can never be entirely abolished – as, for example, is suggested by the often-employed analogy between the exit from the cave and human birth?[20] Maybe the cave is the only place in town, as it were. Does not Plato already speak of the need to return to the cave after exiting it? Where does this (regressive?) desire come from?[21] Or is the cave a purely artificial set-up, an efficient device of domination? If so, who set it up? These questions have in a way always occupied modern philosophy. At its beginning, Descartes dialectized the different options: the Cartesian "cave" is neither a natural human condition (we are not deceived by nature) nor simply cultural (we are not in a metaphorical cave, imprisoned by others' opinions, unable literally to think outside the box). Rather, a *genius malignus*, an evil spirit, constructed a false world that appears completely natural to us. Only by traversing this fantastic cave scenario does Descartes reach a point of absolute certainty (the "I think" about which even an evil cave-maker cannot deceive me). In a way, the early Marx revamps this scenario when he depicts the alienation imposed on human beings by capitalism's *genius malignus* and its disciplinary regime of labor in terms of human prehistory: a state that must be exited through the revolutionary activity of those "who have nothing but their chains."[22] But recall that it can also only be exited because of another shadowy existence, the specter of communism. Alfred Sohn-Rethel implicitly uncovered a connection to the cave allegory in late Marx, claiming that "capitalist relations of productions" are ultimately "a context of delusion in which each thing helps any other to appear normal."[23]

Plato himself presents at least three options of where the (enchainment in the) cave – being fettered in chains and riveted by shadows – originated from: either it is part of our nature, for there is an analogy between the constitution of man's soul and of the state wherein striving for what is rational also always implies struggling with one's inclination toward what is not rational, or it was created by one of the two main enemies of the state, the sophists or the poets. In the tenth book of his *Republic*, Plato criticized not only the poets for generating shadowy representations that capture even the most rational human being (artists in general produce copies of copies that are so enticing that they concur with the real thing, the idea); he also attacks (especially dramatic) poetic art, because there is a danger arising from the practical engagement with imitation, especially when acting. Plato's problem with art as a factory of shadows is not merely epistemological, it is even more practical (similar to ideology in Marx): as soon as one starts imitating someone else, as soon as "[o]ne speaks with the voice of another person . . . one cannot but adopt the identity of this other person." And so "one becomes what one enacts" – one just pretends to do one thing, one thing leads to another, and one ends up doing what one just pretended to do.[24]

Mimesis is infectious, even against better knowledge, and produces a disorienting effect (whereby one loses track of the orientation toward the idea): we know we are just dealing with a mere "fantastic objectivity" (Marx), but it nonetheless starts to affect our inner life. Artistic mimesis is one of Plato's names for a practice that initiates us into a realm of shadowy representation.[25] Equally, the sophists are "enticing image-makers" who "do magic . . . by producing images through words"[26] that capture and direct our thought and action into inconsistent directions. They generate a "mere satisfaction" by presenting shadows of insights, knowledge, and arguments, mere "moving images" that especially capture those unfamiliar with the truth, and thereby, ultimately, "semblance becomes the master over the happiness of human beings."[27] Both produce disorientation in people's practical and theoretical conduct. And we might recall that more recently Badiou partially revamped this criticism when, after the decline of communist states and the worldwide victory of capitalism, he stated that sophists are arising everywhere, pretending to be philosophers,[28] offering fake orientation in political matters and inaugurating a "phony way of thinking."[29] They thereby prevent any real (political) thought from becoming effective – by, inter alia, undermining the distinction between truth and opinion, criminalizing all political action that relies on this distinction, and ultimately not only offering wrong solutions, but – worse – fake problems. And Badiou also repeatedly insisted that one crucial dimension of today's oppression lies in the fact that the universal imperative is to "live without an idea"[30] – which leads to a form of sufferance that is not even experienced as such.

Can Marx be read as presenting a critique of one of the most sophisticated productions of shadows – that is, capitalism? It is important to note that this can imply neither that we should simply distance ourselves from what catches the eye – for such an attitude was reified immediately in the form of cynicism and was turned into a crucial component of the very functioning of the system,[31] a literal "progress in" and through "cynicism"[32] – nor that capitalism's functioning simply relies on an epistemological error. What is important in Marx is not to turn away from economic abstractions (and world-less speculations) and return to the "merely beautiful shadow"[33] of concrete unalienated life. We should also note that the bourgeoisie should not too swiftly be identified as the sole modern conscious cave-makers, since capitalism's logic implies that those who (temporarily) gain from the system are not exempt from its workings (some therefore will speak of a "salaried bourgeoisie"[34] that can lose its privileges at any given moment). All this is part of the reason why Marx does not criticize earlier economists for misrepresenting social relations under capitalism, but instead reads their misrepresentation as the "result of an image of reality that develops independently as a result of the everyday practice of the members of bourgeois society"[35] – an expression of a peculiar capitalist religion of everyday life. It originates in the practical engagement with the "purely fantastic objectivity" of commodities, an objectivity that Marx explicitly describes as "imaginary."[36] He was well aware that, in capitalism, everyone, even capitalists and economists, "succumb to this . . . 'spontaneously' emerging inversion of reality."[37] Everyday practical reality in capitalism entails a constitutive "'religious'," mythical, or "metaphysical moment."[38] This claim concerns all concepts of capitalism's constitutive framework.[39] Even the concepts of labor and labor force that appear as one specific kind of (value generating) commodity in the exchange circle ultimately prove to be shadowy abstractions. For them, it is also the case that "abstractness governs its whole orbit,"[40] whereby there is "absolutely no connection with the physical nature of the commodity and the material relations arising out of [them]."[41]

Marx also clearly saw that an essential part of the functioning of capitalism is the need to create the impression that it is the only, the natural, way of organizing society – he once called this the "eternalization of historic relations of production."[42] Not only does a commodity, by entering into exchange relations, appear to be "endowed with the form of value by nature"[43] – a specific kind of value that seems to be a property of the thing and thus not the result of a specific way of dealing with it – but furthermore capitalism's laws are expressed in the naturalizing "myths and fictions of its ideologists"[44] – precisely those Marx critically engaged with. There is thus a tendency of capitalism to naturalize itself, for example by destroying all traces of pre-capitalist modes of production, but also because the "social forms of production of commodities structure our perception and our thought,"[45] to the extent that, ultimately, a historical social formation becomes "an eternal natural necessity."[46] The challenge presented in this chapter is to read capitalism as a naturalizing realm of shadows (to prepare for the question of how to exit it).

Already, the very first sentence of *Capital* indicated that Marx begins from the idea that "the wealth of societies in which the capitalist mode of production prevails *appears* as an immense collection of commodities,"[47] which then leads him to a formal analysis of the commodity. It is clear that he is referring to a historically specific *appearance* of wealth – economists before him, like Adam Smith, considered wealth to be independent from the form of society in which it existed. *Capital* thus presents us with a critical analysis of capitalism's logic of appearance. In this world, shadowy entities capture and determine those who produce them, since, "just as man is governed in religion by the products of his own brain, so in capitalist production, he is governed by the products of his own hand."[48] These are elements of the "golden chain the wage-labourer has already forged for himself,"[49] expressing the very organizing principles of societies' productive relations that themselves do not appear. Not only are the workers themselves producing the chain that binds them to the system; critically representing the economic laws of movement of modern societies also implies depicting the functioning of this practical self-enchainment.[50] The critical study of the "bewitched, distorted and upside-down world, haunted by Monsieur le Capital and Madame la Terre, who are at the same time social characters and mere things,"[51] the critical engagement with the science that, without understanding it articulates its constitutive assumptions,[52] is therefore similar to what one experiences at "the entrance to hell"[53] – itself, maybe, a very specific kind of cave.

Obviously, the question must be raised – if my hypothesis can be verified – what it means to exit the cave.

How can one conceive of the beginning of emancipation (being freed from the chains) – and who would be freed? What kind of coercion is needed to "force us to think" (Deleuze)? Why is it not enough, as Heidegger noted, to take off the chains for the prisoners to be ready to leave the cave? What must be added to this? How can one even begin to imagine the outside of the cave? What would it mean to leave and then return to the cave, given that, for Plato, the very idea of the good is linked not only to "events"[54] of turn(ing away from the shadows) but also to the return (to the cave)?[55] And what does one do with the problems that occur when one does return – namely, that the other cave prisoners do not want to be liberated? How can one transmit to them what is not knowledge but something else – an idea? Even though I will not be able to answer these questions adequately, I will give some indications of what one needs to take into account in order to give an answer. My starting point is a remark from early Marx which immediately brings to the fore a specific effect of the cave in Plato's description, namely that human beings live in a non- or prehuman state.

In the Cave

Marx writes in his early 1843/44 manuscripts: "[P]olitical economy knows the worker only as a beast of burden, as an animal reduced to the minimum bodily needs [*auf die striktesten Leibesbedürfnisse reduziertes Vieh*]."[56] In political economy – the science that deals with the bourgeois relations of production – there is a reduction of the worker to an animal, to cattle. In passing, Marx here addresses what one may call capitalist animalization of the worker in capitalism.[57] But there is more to this idea than meets the humanist clichéd reading of early Marx. For if capitalism is "the only regime which absolutizes the idea that man is an animal,"[58] does not this reductive operation resemble the setting of Plato's cave? Is this "theory of capitalist subjectivity"[59] analogous to the subjectivity of the cave prisoners? Only a detailed analysis can demonstrate the mysterious, mythical character of this perspective (this perception of the worker may appear entirely natural to an economist, but such transparency is ultimately a semblance) and depict the "moment of distortion"[60] implied in this "fantastic form"[61] of representation. Thus, to answer these questions, it is important to clarify how to conceive of the "reduction" that Marx refers to?

One must note upfront that Marx's claim does not amount to defending the "ridiculous conclusion that we are somehow 'regressing' to the animal level."[62] He does not contend that capitalism implies a sort of evolutionary downgrading whereby everyone would regress to a biological species from a previous evolutionary state. Reduction in Marx must be conceived of not as regressive but as productive.[63] As Fredric Jameson remarked in a different context: "The worker is thus not only reproduced, he is produced in the first place."[64] Capitalism produces the very nature to which it reduces the worker. This indicates a primary goal of the critique of political economy: it demonstrates that the categories of political economy do not simply misrepresent a given objective reality – say, the real social existence of the worker – but that political economy is generative of a reality of its own. This is not simply to say that all categories of political economy do not have a real-world equivalent and are mere fictions that receive a scientific articulation in a

scientific superstructural apparatus. Rather, the entities
that political economy refers to are part of a class-biased
creation of social reality itself. "[T]here is no 'objective
social reality' which is not already mediated by political
subjectivity";[65] in the world(view) of the bourgeoisie,
any worker is reduced to an animal. This is why Marx
criticizes the bourgeois system and its political economy,
which creates a reality in which there actually exists
such a worker.[66] The "worker" in this sense is a real
abstraction, the "result of a preceding [even though not
conscious] abstraction"[67] that constitutes it. This means
that for the critique of political economy, "all categories
the text [*Capital*, but the same holds for the early Marx's
text] had analyzed ... had involved class struggle."[68]
The reduced worker is a class-specific representation of
the "worker" – a representation that is at the same time
formative of the very reality that it describes.

For Marx's claim, this must mean that the natural
state to which the worker is reduced is always already
a state of second nature.[69] This does not simply imply
that, for Marx, the worker simply became a domesticated
animal. Although one reads in *Capital* that "[i]n the
earliest period of human history, domesticated animals,
i.e. animals that have undergone modification by means
of labour, play the chief part as instruments of labour
along with stones, wood, bones and shells, which have
also had work done on them,"[70] the reduction Marx
refers to is not a domestication of the human species
by means of labor. Otherwise one could claim that man
becomes human by means of labor, but it could not be
claimed that the worker, by means of labor within political economy, is turned into an animal. Domestication
generates a second nature, but the formation of a second

nature does not as such imply a reduction. Marx's words, rather, imply that political economy reverses an effect of the earliest periods of human history. If one is in any way dealing here with an effect of domestication, it needs to be different from "the importance of domesticated animals for the beginning of civilization."[71] One is instead faced with a domestication that entails historical reduction, not progression; one that ensures the perpetuation and reproduction of the established order without any civilizing element. If one is here dealing with domestication, it is uncivilizing, dehistoricizing. How does such a peculiar operation of productive reduction, of reductive production, work?

Surplus Abstraction

Political economy knows the worker only as an animal. Capitalism thereby seems to become a gigantic zoo filled with "dehumanized creature(s)";[72] a wildlife that comprises the "boundless reproduction of animals individually weak and constantly hunted down."[73] But capitalism is not nature. It is instructive to proceed here by recourse to another operation on which capitalist political economy constitutively relies, namely abstraction.[74] How capitalist reductionism and the theory of abstraction are linked becomes clearer when Marx states: "It is true that eating, drinking and procreating, etc., are also genuine human functions. However, when abstracted from other aspects of human activity and turned into final and exclusive ends, they are animal."[75] The reduction of the worker to an animal is grounded in a previous act of abstracting functions from the human life form. Abstraction is thus already, for the early Marx, a crucial category of political economy. At first sight, it seems to be reductive because stripping off certain functions from their human form implies a moment of un-forming, of deformation. Yet, even though abstraction de-civilizes, it does not ignore the concrete function. Rather, it essentializes one particular aspect of the particular. It takes one concrete determination, singles it out, and hypostatizes it into the essential feature of the particular bearer of this function; it takes some particular (function), divests it of its general form – of its (human) context – and essentializes the particular character of this particularity. Abstraction particularizes the general essence of a particular thing (of the worker in this case) by essentializing a particular aspect of its concrete particularity, which is why abstraction implies an essentializing particularization of the particular.[76]

In face of a concrete particularity, abstraction accentuates the very form of its particularity, neglecting all that is universal in it. But reduction occurs precisely when this form is turned into being the essence of the particularity, positing the form of the particular (that is, one function) as the sole universal determination. Reduction takes place when the particularized particular is itself posited as a new essence, as a new (universal) genus. One should add here that a process of abstraction never appears "unless it is somehow made to be a thing in its own right"[77] – and is thus linked to reduction. What is reductively made into a genus is the monstrous worker-animal. There is thus no objective "worker" in (objective) reality; instead, "worker" is a signifier delineating a specific subject-position. In other words, the worker is not a "biologically given" entity, "but a socially produced one."[78]

So, what does it mean to think abstractly? Abstract thought in general is particularizing, particularized, since it fundamentally relies on the abstract distinction between abstract and concrete thought. This distinction turns both sides into being merely particular and makes it impossible for abstraction (as only one of the two possibilities) ever to be universal.[79] Yet, abstraction nonetheless engrosses universality by inverting and redoubling its own determination: if there are only particularities (due to the abstract distinction between abstraction and concretion), then there are only particularities and there is thus only abstraction. Therefore, abstraction leads to reduction: totalizing and hypostatizing its own particularity entails an operation of essentialization (of its own abstract presuppositions).[80] Abstraction becomes reductive when the particularization it entails is totalized and thereby essentialized. It is essentialized when it is itself posited not only as all there is, but also as a particular new, seemingly concrete entity (as "worker," for example). There is reduction more specifically when one abstractly relates to an operation of abstraction and essentializes a particular aspect of a particular object, creating a new object out of it – the shadow of an object. Reduction always implies an abstraction from the very act of abstraction, a redoubling of abstraction. Reduction is surplus abstraction.

Redoubled abstraction generates a reductive surplus. Through abstraction, particular human functions are taken to be nothing but particular functions; abstraction accentuates the very form of particularity of the particular (function). If these functions are then identified with the worker as such, with what he is, there is reductive essentialization. This operation thus produces a new genus. Political economy knows the worker only as an animal, yet this animal is a truly particular animal, it is a surplus abstraction. In this peculiar representation, political economy's relation to the worker becomes manifest, since it knows him only as an animal. This knowledge is abstract knowledge. But it is effectively reductive because political economy abstractly relates to the abstract concept of the worker it itself produced. This surplus of abstraction is what makes political economy reductive and its knowledge of the workers productive of strange animals that are not only domesticated by it but, rather, brought into being. The animal that the worker is, is a doubly abstract entity, an imaginary ideological excrescence of political economy. The peculiar animal that the worker is for political economy does not exist (there is no "*sujet supposé de l'histoire*"[81]) and he is hence even less than an (ordinary) animal. We here "confront a form of 'naked life' far more deeply rooted in the economic system itself than Agamben's hopeless inhabitants of the concentration camps."[82] This unnatural entity manifests an excess of abstraction constitutive for political economy, as if its "consumed [*verzehrte*] nature rises into a new ideal shape as a realm of shadow."[83] The worker is for political economy an un-animal (which is neither animal nor human, but which opens up a third dimension, undermining the choice between human and animal). Even though this un-animal – *Untier* in German – is unnatural, it is nonetheless presented as a natural being, as animal. This generates the ultimate force of reductive essentialization, essentializing reduction which is a *modus operandi* of real abstraction.

Now a Stomach, Now an Anus . . .

Political economy knows the worker only as an un-animal. Yet, it is presented as a natural entity. It is reduced and produced animality, presented so that "the worker" names the sum of his isolated particular bodily functions. For political economy, the worker is what it assumes he has: he is what he has and what he has is his body; the worker and his bodily functions form an identity. As Badiou argued: "[I]n order to validate the equation 'existence = individual = body', contemporary doxa [in capitalism] must valiantly reduce humanity to an over-stretched [and reduced] vision of animality."[84] For the worker, there are only bodies and functions. Reductive abstraction essentializes, and what it essentializes is the identity of being and having. In capitalism, one thus witnesses a naturalization of (redoubled) abstraction. The worker is seen as an animal because the animal knows no distinction between having and being, it is "immediately one with its life activity," "it is that activity."[85] For the worker, therefore, "all the physical and intellectual senses have been replaced by the simple estrangement of all these senses – the sense of having."[86] Everything in the worker's life – his subjective position in and generated by capitalism – everything that he is, is reduced to the sense of having. Political economy knows the worker only as an apparent body, immediately identical with its functions and needs (at one with his life activity). And these can be reduced to a minimum; this "reduces the labourers to 'mere animal conditions of existence'."[87]

However, for Marx the worker is not only reduced to his existing biological body. In political economy, even his bodily unity is abstract, since it is the sum of its

isolated particular bodily functions; it is a further product of abstracting reduction. This is what Marx has in
mind when he writes that in capitalism a working being
"becomes an abstract activity and a stomach."[88] A working individual therefore becomes a peculiar (animal-)
dividual, a divided animal, a fragile conglomerate of
his particularized bodily functions. The worker is rep-
resented as if he were once a stomach, a penis, a throat,
etc. This "animal, by its bodily structure, finds itself emi-
nently apt to the functioning of its body, and outside the
functioning of its body, it can do nothing."[89] It is torn
between particular isolated functions. The reduction of
the man to a surplus abstraction generates "an anar-
chism of the immediate, a disaggregation of the corporeal
and cerebral systems into vanishing abstractions."[90] One
might here see a parallel to Freud's depiction of infantile
sexuality: whereas in normal and perverted sexuality "a
well-organized tyranny has been established . . . infantile
sexuality . . . lacks, speaking generally, any such centering
and organization; its separate component instincts have
equal rights, each of them goes its own way to obtain-
ing pleasure."[91] The worker is hence treated as being
without centering, without organization, in some sense
as a child, which constantly needs to be commanded.[92]
This is because the worker is not simply interpellated
as an animal, but, by being an essential element of the
exchange processes of capitalist relations of production (the worker has to sell his "labor force"), he has to
assume a position that is also full of theological niceties
and is thus also determined by the form (as commodity)
in which he appears. He is for political economy nothing
more than the "loose coupling"[93] of his particular bodily
functions, "an animal convinced that the law of the body

harbours the secret of hope,"[94] "degrade[d] . . . to a frag-
ment of man [*Teilmenschen*]."[95] The consciousness that
political economy thereby assigns to the worker equals
what Hegel called sense-certainty: there is an alleged
certainty of the "now"-instance in which the worker has,
and hence is, a certain bodily function or satisfies a particular bodily need, and this is what reduces the worker.
He is certain to be the one he is, when he senses that
he has a particular need or bodily function. This is the
naturalized outcome of the reductive fragmentation.

For political economy, the worker is now a mouth,
now an anus; now the eating, now the digestion, now
the excretion, etc. Hegel has shown that sense-certainty
cannot but run into contradictions, which can be condensed into a one-liner: as soon as I say "now," now is
not now anymore. For Marx's argument, this means
that the worker is identified with a process of a vanishing of one "now" into another, which is repeated until
the vanishing itself vanishes (and the worker dies). In
some sense the worker lives as if already dead – "*le mort
saisit le vif!*"[96] – structurally vanishing but constantly
resurrected by the labor process, which "awaken[s]" him,
as well as certain materials, "from the dead, change[s]
them from merely possible into real and effective use-
values," "bath[ing them] in the fire of labour"; it "raises
the means of production from the dead merely by entering into contact with them, infus[ing] them with life."[97]
Political economy's reductive production generates an
entity that is made of continually vanishing abstractions ("nows") enlivened by the omnipresent coercion
to work. The essentializing identity of being and having
leads to the fact that the worker is structurally already
vanished, he is inexistent: he is the vanishing of his

vanishing functions. As this vanishing, his only end in a society in which there is such reductive production lies in vanishing – ontologically, historically, politically, but also economically behind what he produces. The worker animal is an unnatural animal, and political economy thus transforms man's "advantage over animals . . . into the disadvantage that his inorganic body, nature, is taken from him."[98] His nature is vanishing nature, naturalized vanishing. Because he is considered to be an animal – that is, as identical with its life activity – the worker is an animal whose nature is to vanish, is vanishing. This is why he is less than an animal, the shadow of an agent. Different from the setting in Plato's cave, one can see here that even those who appear to be the cave prisoners, the workers, are ultimately shadowy entities. This gives a different twist to Engels's claim that "from the moment the bourgeoisie emerged . . . it was always accompanied by its shadow, the proletariat."[99]

The worker dismembered into the "now"-instances of his particular functions (particularization of the particular) has this dismemberment for his essence (reduction). He is a "stunted monster,"[100] an un-animal. If the only sense lies in having and what he has is constantly vanishing, his sole end is therefore to lose what he has (already lost). Any other end does not "exist any longer, not only not in a human form, but rather it exists in an inhuman form, therefore not even in an animal form."[101] Since "it is not only human needs which . . . [this] . . . man lacks – even his animal needs cease to exist."[102] The worker is an animal deprived of its animality. For he never had this animality. The worker-animal is the surplus of redoubled abstraction.

The Immanence of Reduction, or:
Lacking (Animal) Lack

How does this affect the worker? One should recall that the capitalist organization of production necessarily generates a spatial condensation of the multiplicity of workers into a cooperative collective "single force" in the modern factory system (which in principle remains pertinent even today). This condensation "begets . . . a rivalry and a stimulation of the 'animal spirits', which heighten the efficiency of each individual worker":[103] such working conditions allow for a spontaneous ideology of the sole survival of the fittest. Working under capitalist conditions, everyone thereby becomes filled by the "Furies of private interest,"[104] being an appendix of a "mechanical monster whose body fills the whole factory"[105] of society – a monster of which "the workers are merely conscious organs"[106] that are conscious because they know they are executing the interest of someone else for the sake of their own interest. This indicates a structural perversion: the worker becomes the mere instrument of another whose will he realizes because "the fact that the worker can do anything at all with their abilities seems to be a result brought about by capital."[107]

So, what then is "the worker's side of the story"?[108] Marx states that "the result is that man feels that he is acting freely only in his animal functions – eating, drinking, and procreating, or at most in his dwelling and adornment – while in his human function he is nothing more than an animal. The animal becomes the human and the human becomes the animal."[109] This indicates one structural origin of leisure time. When the worker labors he feels unfree, but he feels free when he fucks, drinks, and eats in his "free" time. This time structurally allows for consumerist enjoyment. But it is this model of freedom that leads the worker himself deeper into what he sought to free himself from, namely in the identification of freedom with the now-instances of his bodily functions. When the "now" (of leisure, the hoped-for weekend) passes, he stops being free (and needs to work again). But if this "now" of freedom has always already passed over into another "now" (of labor), then freedom is always already in the past for him. Freedom is the permanently vanishing delay of the return to labor.[110]

To the extent that the abstract past of the human is the animal (the abstract idea of a previous biological state), so the worker conceives of his freedom as something that abstractly passes and ultimately is always already past. The worker lives in (t)his past, conceiving of his freedom as the passing and hence as the past of his freedom, which in abstract terms is the animal. Political economy thus implies a peculiar economy of time. The worker lives, embodies, and subjectivizes the reductive abstraction brought forth by bourgeois political economy.[111] Capitalism is not simply a modernizing revolutionary force, but constitutively relies on the regression and reductive production of premodern, prehuman elements, the "worker" in its political economy being one of its most prominent names. Against this background one can understand late Marx's claim: "The organization of the capitalist process of production, once it is fully developed, breaks down all resistance."[112] The reason for this is that the complex operations of abstraction that entail reduction and unfreedom are self-deceivingly experienced by the worker as freedom[113] – the "worker" always already being a product of the capitalist system.

The assumption that the working class just needs to awaken is flawed from the very beginning.

One can recall here Althusser's definition of ideology (the imaginary relation to one's real conditions of existence): the way in which the worker understands his freedom perpetuates and reproduces the very reduction that political economy performs. The worker is living in, and as, reductive naturalized abstraction; he (imaginarily) feels whole and natural in his (real) dividedness and reductive artificiality. He is a shadow (of capitalist's political economy) since his essence (freedom) is a mere shadow. Capitalism interpellates workers by addressing them precisely as subjects that are nothing but shadows of freedom, as nothings who therefore should strive to become all through their engagement in the market (as if a reification of the famous line from the *International*). The object of political economy's knowledge and the worker's self-understanding therefore become exchangeable. They coincide, since the worker assumes that his freedom lies precisely in the reduced moments of his existence and thereby confirms the firm grip that political economy has on him. Hegel once claimed: "If that which lacks something does not at the same time stand above its lack, the lack is not for it a lack. An animal is lacking from our point of view, not from its own."[114] The limitations of the animal are thus objective limitations. The unnatural animal – the worker – acts like an animal, since he experiences his unfreedom as freedom. He thus does not recognize his own limitations as limitations: in his relation to his reduced existence, he does not (imaginarily) perceive the lack (of being reduced to the temporal instances of his bodily functions) as lack. He thereby identifies with his reduction to an animal. But this means that the worker even loses the lack that the animal still has; the animal has a lack, because it lacks the knowledge of its own limitations. The worker is less than an animal because he loses the knowledge that he has of his lack and thereby lacks even lacking the animal-way. The worker is not the proprietor of his own lack.

This paradoxical insight becomes more intelligible if one recalls Hegel's claim stating that "man is an animal, but even in his animal functions he does not remain within the in-itself as the animal does, but becomes conscious of the in-itself . . . and raises it . . . into self-conscious science. . . because he knows that he is an animal, he ceases to be an animal."[115] Man has the knowledge of his own limitations, that is, of himself being an animal. Yet this very knowledge makes him into more than an animal. But as soon as this happens, the knowledge of him being an animal is falsified (due to his very knowledge, he became more than an animal). But man does not know that the knowledge he has is now false knowledge, whereby he again regresses to animality (not knowing his limitations). But then again, his knowledge (of him being an animal) converts into adequate knowledge and he again ceases to be an animal. For Hegel, man is this constant oscillation between man and animal, the parallax of inadequate and adequate knowledge. This means that man is not just one side of the human–animal distinction; he is, rather, the very split that enables this distinction, the identity of the identity and difference of man and animal. Put in different terms: there is no relation between man and animal, but there is such a thing as a human animal, which is the incorporation of this non-relation.

Relating this back to Marx, this means that the worker

knows his limitations, he knows he is not what political economy assumes he is, but he does not know that he knows it, or knows very well but acts nonetheless as if he does not know. Thereby he starts to lack "more" than the animal;[116] he even lacks the lack the animal has – there is an unconscious lack. The animal is limited, the human knows that it is limited and hence stands above its limitations; the un-animal limits itself (being subjectivized as worker) and does not know that it knows that it does so. The worker is reduced to an un-animal, because he knows he is only an animal but he does not know what he knows. Marx depicts this as follows:

> Conscious life activity directly distinguishes man from animal life activity. Only because of that is he a species being. Or rather, he is a conscious being, i.e. his own life is an object for him, only because he is a species-being. Only because of that is his activity free activity. Estranged labour [in capitalism] reverses the relationship.[117]

This is to say that political economy reverses, perverts, the form of human life activity by transforming conscious life activity into unconscious un-life – a life that does not live – activity.[118] The worker does not know what he knows and he therefore acts as if he were nothing – but an animal.

Obscured Reduction and Abstract Naturalization

Political economy knows the worker only as an animal – but as one that de facto has a peculiar non-animality as its essence. A text with which Marx initially planned to close the first volume of *Capital* offers another instructive take on the animal–man distinction:

Man is distinguished from all other animals by the limitless
and flexible nature of his needs. But it is equally true that no
animal is able to restrict his needs to the same unbelievable
degree and to reduce the conditions of his life to the absolute minimum. In a word, there is no animal with the same
talent for "Irishing" himself.[119]

The worker for political economy is less than an
animal; he is this absolute minimum of life activity. Here
the potential reduction is what defines man. Man is the
only animal that can be less than an animal.[120] Animal
needs know objective minima, precisely because animals do not know their limitation. But man is an entity
whose substance and whose needs are plastic, because
what one knows (say, one's limits) one can redetermine.
Knowing no objective limit, he is able to become less and
less. His minimum is subjective and thus up for limitless redetermination. Man is the only animal that can
therefore live at an absolute minimum; only man can live
as if he does not live – this is the worker. But here lies the
dialectical catch: if political economy knows the worker
only as an animal, and hence reduces him, this reduction relies on what is properly human and not animal.
Political economy, in reducing man to an animal, refers
in the act of reduction to man in his specific human
quality.

Political economy can only reduce the worker to an
animal, which is less than an animal, because man
will always already have been a *"voided* animal"[121] –
an animal without any (animal) substance proper. The
worker is, then, for political economy, nothing but that
entity, which can be infinitely reduced, because he
has nothing whose substance could not be infinitely

reduced.[122] The problem with the reductive operation of political economy lies in the fact that it assumes that its reductive knowledge of the worker is nonetheless – although there is a subjective reduction in the double sense of the term – objective knowledge, that is, a knowledge of a given object, the worker, whose objectivity is considered to lie in the natural(ized) identity with his (given) particularized body. By considering the outcome of its own reduction to a given natural object, "given" in the form of a natural animal body, political economy obscures and conceals its own act of reduction.

In *Capital*, Marx depicts value-producing labor in its most elementary form (mere human labor) as "the expenditure of simple labour-power, i.e. of the labour-power possessed in his [the worker's] bodily organism by every ordinary man, on the average, without being developed in any special way."[123] Political economy assumes that the worker is in possession of his particular bodily functions, which are taken to be preconditions for labor in general. They are what the worker uses when working, and "worker" is thereby the name of the proprietor of this power (labor force). This identification naturalizes because it generates the assumption that the equation "worker = animal" is a natural one and thus not an equation. This is why the "worker" is treated as a proprietor of his particularized bodily function. The worker is reductively determined as animal body and his freedom is therefore identified with a given capacity of (using) his property, namely his body. But what is also naturalized is the very concept (and the relations) of property on which political economy constitutively relies. Political economy, by obscuring its own act of reduction, naturalizes itself abstractly, producing reductive nature. It makes itself into a natural environment whose sole (un-) natural inhabitant is the worker-animal.

Yet, late Marx claims, when analyzing money, "it is as if, alongside and external to lions, tigers, rabbits, and all other actual animals, which form when grouped together the various kinds, species, subspecies, families, etc. of the animal kingdom, there existed in addition the animal, the individual incarnation of the entire animal kingdom."[124] Money is the only true animal,[125] the true incarnation of all the species of the animal kingdom brought about by a process of abstraction. This is because political economy in this way naturalizes at the same time the abstract exchangeability of all particularities that find what they have in common expressed in an indifferent abstract third: the animal, money. That there is a universal equivalent means that all particularities have something in common, namely the form of particularity. Reductive acts of abstraction generate through the practice of exchange something new, the money-form, on which they seem to rely in the first place.[126] This also provides the basis on which the "worker" and the outcome of political economy's reduction become exchangeable. If he works for money, what it pays for is precisely what political economy reductively assumes he needs, and thus is. The animal kingdom of political economy thereby establishes an abstract exchangeability of the reductive abstraction ("worker") and the un-animal that it names. The most basic of all operations of naturalization of political economy – a self-naturalization – thus concerns the very idea of exchangeability (of whatever shadowy terms and entities).

The capitalist political economy – in its self-representation – in its necessary form of appearance, the "world market," provides "the very basis and the living atmosphere,"[127] the best environment for the animal. And by making this fact fully transparent (the worker is only in capitalism regarded as an animal), it also obscures it: the abstract name "worker" is presented as a unity of the reductive fragmented bodily functions that he is supposed to be, as a ground that abstractly unifies the endless succession of particular nows of the bodily functions whose natural proprietor the worker is (postulated to be) and whose natural environment is the market. Such naturalization also affects temporality, for time is understood as the succession of "now"-instances, in which there is an objective given bodily function. This implies that time as such disappears, since the future of the particular function will be the repetition of its past. The future of the worker is hence the particularity of his past (the animal), which means (1) that the worker is already living in his future, in a reproduction of the past and (2) that the present (of time) disappears: "there has been history, there is no longer any."[128] Time via naturalization does not simply become natural time but rather the time of nature, which implies the abolition of (historical) time. From this one can see why Marx refers to capitalism as a pre-history of mankind.

Getting Used To It

Bourgeois political economy thinks reductively. How can workers continually live with this "downward synthe-sis,"[129] as political economy's un-animal? One answer is, because they can get used to it: "The advance of capitalist production develops a working class which by educa-tion, tradition and habit looks upon the requirements of that mode of production as self-evident natural laws."[130] And even the effective value proportions "established by a social process that goes on behind the back of the producers" – Heinrich speaks of a "universal background lighting"[131] provided by fetishism (recall the cave setting) – "appear to the producers to have been handed down by tradition."[132] But what does it mean to get used to something? Reduction does not comprise regressing to a given first nature. Since political economy's operation of reduction is productive, one always deals with second nature. And second nature is conceptually synonymous with habit.

For Hegel, habit does not only fulfill a formative and educative function; it is also crucial for the objective constitution of sociopolitical life.[133] Through habit, human nature is transformed "into a second, spiritual nature, and [it] makes this spiritual level habitual to them."[134] Yet this very anthropological revolution relies on two interwoven momentums, namely mechanism and freedom: there is what Hegel calls "the mechanism of self-feeling"[135] – that is, the production of a mechanism. An activity is repeated in a purely mechanical manner, a repetition without consciousness of repetition. If one learns a new language, one must be habituated to (mechanically) reproduce certain syntactical rules, the vocabulary, etc. Mechanical repetition is the very precondition for free self-expression, and generates a specific self-feeling, namely, that I cannot imagine myself without this habit. What at first seems to be the opposite of freedom (mechanism) thus turns out to be its precondition.[136] The concatenation of a mechanism (having become unconscious) that grounds freedom and conscious freedom relying on mechanical repetition makes it possible that a subject "has or moves in its determinations."[137] But mechanism is a precondition of freedom only "as long as we have habits and not just are our habits."[138] Habit always comes with the danger that its mechanical side takes over.

> The ruse of habit . . . can reveal itself as the curse of habit: To the extent that habit becomes mechanical through and through and absorbs the whole soul . . . The most radical expression that Hegel gives to this aspect of habit is . . . that the habit of living if it becomes totally abstract "is death itself."[139]

Against this background one can see how the reduction performed by political economy implies turning the precondition of freedom (mechanism) into the very actuality of freedom. Reductively, mechanism is identified with freedom by essentializing the abstract identity between being and having. The worker becomes the second nature he has. There is only a pure mechanical self-relation left: he is stuck with the forced choice between freedom as mechanism of labor and freedom as mechanism of bodily functions (which have become exchangeable). He experiences his freedom in what he has, and what he has is mechanism(s). Hegel once stated: "The universal and objective element in work . . . lies in the process of abstraction . . . The abstraction of production makes work more and more mechanical, until finally the human being is able to step aside and let a machine take his place."[140] Marx twists this claim: the worker is not simply replaced by a machine, but is turned into a mechanism, reduced to the mechanical side of habit. This is why he can also state that political economy operates "[b]y reducing the worker's need to the barest and most miserable level of physical subsistence, and by reducing his activity to the most abstract mechanical movement."[141] The worker is reduced to mechanical movement – like a Cartesian animal – by making having a and being this habit indistinguishable; a "stunted monster produced by overwork in the mechanical monotony" of capitalism.[142] Hegel claimed that "only man gets as far as grasping himself in this complete abstraction of the I."[143] This means that only man can reduce himself to this mechanism.

Yet, the analysis of reduction is not complete if another element is not also taken into account. Marx notes that "if money is the bond which ties me to human life and society to me, which links me to nature and to man, is money not the bond of all bonds? . . . It is the true agent of separation and the true cementing agent, it is the chemical power of society."[144] This passage indicates how the process of reduction is linked to the very nature of capitalism, since what mediates the worker's own separation from his own freedom is a separating as well as a binding chemical power. What binds together these multiplicities of abstract mechanical movements (the workers reduced to un-animals) is analogous to chemical interaction. Hence, capitalist nature (the naturalized produced and perpetuated reductions) can be understood as composite of mechanism and chemism: a chemical power grounding and keeping together the reduction of laboring subjects to abstract objective mechanical movements: capitalism = chemism + mechanism. What to make of this? Marx depicts how the worker is reduced to an animal, precisely because his functions are "abstracted from other aspects of human activity and turned into final and exclusive ends, they are animal."[145] It is precisely the idea of transforming abstracted functions into ends in themselves that here offers a key to understanding the concatenation of mechanism and chemism. Since neither is simply a natural science model applied to sociopolitical relations, but, rather, a different model of how to conceive of an end. The political economy of capitalism hence entails two (reductive) ways of conceptualizing the "end." What is at stake is what it means for one's whole existence to be exhausted by ends immanent to an unnatural form of un-life.[146] By linking mechanistic and chemist explanations, the political economy of capitalism reduces the universal idea of proper subjective ends.

Capitalist Nature/Anabasis

Near the end of Hegel's *Logic of Science* one finds a detailed discussion of two (ultimately problematic) ways of positing (subjective) ends: mechanism and chemism.[147] Mechanistic explanations start from the assumption that there is nothing but objects. What moves objects are other objects and relations between objects are understood in terms of one object affecting and moving another. Subjects in mechanism are also objects of movements – their ends are imposed by other objects. The end (of an action) can only be thought of by recourse to one object's force on another. Hegel then states that mechanism always entails a "striving for totality":[148] mechanism seeks to totalize itself and thus claims that there are only objects and nothing else. But here the conceptual problem emerges: mechanism is driven to totalize itself; all there is are objects and their external relation to another. But then it can no longer properly individuate the objects it refers to and ends up with only one object (which is a problem, as it needs at least two distinct objects to upholds its own claim), but it can also no longer account for why it itself (as a theoretical position) exists. All there is, says mechanism, are objects and their relations, but it is itself not an object. It thereby assumes that there is something external to objects and their relations and ends up by embodying itself in a concept of "end" that stands in contradiction to what it explicitly conceptualizes as "end."

Chemist explanations seek to avoid this problem. They assume that there are immanent causes to entities, which make them move – and a chemist position explains why it itself exists by recourse to chemism. Ends here are specific to those entities that are driven by them. It thereby seems to subjectivize the objects of mechanism – from mere outer objective ends, to ends immanent to a non-object. But if there is something inside me moving me, I can only relate to it if it can become an object of my will. In chemism this is not the case; although what drives me is internal, it always remains external to me. It is an immanent externality (even though it is more than just external causality). A chemical end is one that determines me internally, but I can nonetheless never influence it, as I will never directly encounter it (for example, how long my fingers grow is beyond the grasp of my will). Positing such a type of end is to assume natural necessity, even if it is different from mechanism (chemism is a version of Aristotelianism) – but one thereby attains a concept of "end" that is ultimately also contradictory: it is an end that is posited as always already immanently given, thus as not posited. Chemism denies the act of positing an end by positing it (and thereby itself) as not posited (as naturally given).

This starkly abbreviated account of Hegel's argument, the concatenation of chemism and mechanism that makes capitalist nature, can be resumed as follows: there is something beyond the individual's reach (the chemical power), which inherently drives them into the reductive and reifying identification of being and having an end (into mechanism[149]). On one side, there is a loss of individuation and therewith of even conceiving of an end; on the other there is the assumption that there is an end that never has been posited and thus is always already there by nature. The reductive and reproductive movement of capital becomes the internal end of all subjective actions, determining them externally from the inside, driving them to embrace mechanism. The guiding orientations of subjective action are mere shadows of orientation; its realizations of freedom are shadows of it, since the bourgeoisie "has resolved personal worth into exchange value, and in place of the numberless indefeasible chartered freedoms, has set up that single, unconscionable freedom – Free Trade."[150] Mechanism and chemism are ways of rendering the very concept of the end so that it turns into natural necessity and abolishes true subjective actions.

The mechanist and the chemist logic of ends are components of capitalism's logic, making its functioning appear as if it were a natural necessity. Not because capitalism is a natural necessity, but because it tends to naturalize itself through mechanical and chemist renderings of what an end is and thereby constantly creates unnatural entities. How does this naturalizing action of capitalism's structure relate to the famous description from the *Manifesto* that "the bourgeoisie cannot exist without constantly revolutionizing" its social formation, playing the "most revolutionary part" in permanently modernizing society and pushing forward a process whose product is "an incoherent mass" of workers?[151] How does naturalization and this kind of revolution work together? Recall that Marx clearly stated that, with capitalism, "[t]he prehistory of human society . . . closes."[152] What seems to be the driving force of historical development – even though and because it abolishes temporality proper – is a non-and prehistorical social formation. This is, inter alia, because it can only work by constantly producing shadowy prehuman (un-animal) agents and by permanently regressing to premodern forms of domination.[153] There is a permanent and literal "revolution" taking place just to not revolutionize anything – a transformation without transformation – and to eternalize the structural status quo. What does this mean for the reading hypothesis of the present chapter? Does Marx's critique amount to re-actualizating, remodeling, the myth of the cave?

If one were to equate cave prisoners to workers, one is led to the surprising conclusion that the prisoners are themselves shadows – and are a crucial part of reproducing the very constitutive operators of the cave. The workers as shadows are those captured and enchained by what they themselves assume to be, produce, and carry to the market (even if their commodities tell them to do so). In Marx's critique of this category, we also thus find a "theory of the illusion necessary to the capitalist [and the worker] for him to occupy his place as agent of production, as bearer of the capitalist relation."[154] In this sense, the "worker" does not name any privileged emancipatory position – it rather (at least potentially) names the lure to assume such a position and provides the ground for reifying the inexistent nothing that the worker is so that he is constantly confronted with the imperative: you are nothing, strive to (become and) own all! There is thus no alienated substance of the worker behind the un-animal[155] by which he is presented and which one could regain. It is rather through capitalism's logic of shadows that more shadows emerge, inter alia the shadow of rich concrete real life behind or outside the constitutive abstractions. Shadows multiply.

Marx's depiction also indicates that capitalism's political economy constructs something structurally comparable to Plato's mythic cave: in it – this is part of its naturalizing tendency – temporality is absorbed into space. With the disappearance of history and temporality proper (through self-naturalization), there is only a specific kind of space, the capitalist globe, "the world interior of capital."[156] This world interior is one "in which the economic objects are related and together manifest social processes while concealing them."[157] Its world is "precisely the space in which the determinations of the structure manifest themselves (the space of phantasmagoric objectivity)."[158] There is thus no longer a world proper – only the cupola that capitalism creates in its process of "globalization," only a mystification, a shadow of the world; and there is no subject supposed to revolutionize it; again, only the shadow of a subject, but not a subject that is supposed to see (through) the shadows. Its world is the shadow of a world. This itself sounds like quite a fatalist – and exaggerated – version of Plato's allegory. What could it mean to turn the gaze therein?[159] One way of reading the critique of political economy against this background is that it helps to turn the gaze. Not to the real sites of production, not to the concrete life behind the abstraction, but to see that "there is nothing to be seen" behind the shadow "unless we go behind it ourselves."[160] In other words, what one can learn from the critique of political economy is that (even redoubled) abstractions can generate a (shadow of a) world – even though many did not ask "the question why this content has assumed that particular form"[161] (to use one of Marx's famous formulations). One should recall that Hegel refers to the domain tackled in his *Science of Logic*, in the book Marx is implicitly referring to with his recourse to the linkage of mechanism and chemism, as a "realm of shadows,"[162] which is strictly distinct from merely empty abstractions. In short, even with shadows, it holds: one splits into two. Not only does Hegel's book, almost at its end, traverse the concepts of mechanism and chemism to proceed to a proper understanding of what it means to posit an end (Hegel calls this "teleology"), but afterwards he also argues, like Plato, that to do so one must have an (absolute) idea. And is Marx not silently pointing out that this is the way to go?

The Science of Logic demonstrates that pure thought cannot but operate with pure shadows that are entirely subtracted from any concrete referent, but it also depicts that this seemingly shallow medium in the end leads to the proper creation of a world: it depicts the thought of God "before the creation"[163] and the book ends not only with the concept of the idea, but also at a point where this very creation ends (whether complete or not) and becomes actual. One can thus see that there is a way that leads from the realm of shadows to something real that is not outside the realm of shadows, but is a Real realm of the shadows themselves.[164] It indicates a different use of shadows, a different, materialist practice of shadows that is able to generate a world; and, as Hegel clearly demonstrates, to understand what it means to be free – as free as God was before the creation – is to understand what it means to pass through the laborious steps of the shadows (that is, concepts).[165] Might one not draw from this the conclusion that to properly answer the question of how to turn the gaze, of how to exit and then return to today's reductive cave of shadows, one should start – and maybe this is just the first step – by turning one's head and returning from Marx to Hegel? Some have argued that the critique of political economy (or any other kind of critique) will never be able to provide us with an idea of what is to be done; and maybe turning from Marx to Hegel (not in order to replace him, but to return to him via the latter) will provide the means if not to break the spell of capitalism's peculiarly dis- and re-enchanted nature, at least to understand what it could mean that the human being "wins its truth only when, in utter dismemberment it finds itself."[166]

3

Imprinting Negativity: Hegel Reads Marx

"... to draw Philosophy out of the solitude into which it has wandered – to do such work as this we may hope that we are called by the higher spirit of our time."

Hegel

Let us begin with common sense: capital's logic of development is based on just one goal, that of profit maximization, with no regard for how its speculative movement affects society (at the global level).[1] But does this self-development of capital, disregarding the structural changes in the social reality itself, reach its limits at one point of its development, or does it go on forever? Global late capitalism[2] generates a series of antagonisms and contradictions, which are unable to be resolved within its social form. Ultimately, it is becoming clear that these antagonisms and contradictions will put an end to its constant reproduction; what is unclear, however, is whether or not the end of capitalism will also entail the end of the world.

The political as well as the philosophical challenge

today is to consider not only the form in which capitalist reproduction might be brought to a halt, but to think also of how the challenges posed by the contemporary form of capitalist development hinder or condition any systemic social change. That is to say, how are we to think about the social changes and transformations caused by capital in the entire social field, from the changed status of labor, to the crisis of the working class, "immaterial" capital, ecological catastrophes, new technological inventions, *homo sacer*, etc.?

According to Slavoj Žižek, in thinking our way out of capitalism, we have to bear in mind that:

> it is not enough simply to remain faithful to the communist Idea; one has to locate within historical reality antagonisms which give this Idea a practical urgency. The only true question today is: do we endorse the predominant naturalization of capitalism, or does today's global capitalism contain antagonisms which are sufficiently strong to prevent its indefinite reproduction?

Based on this, he enumerates four such antagonisms, which he names as "four riders of apocalypse."

> the looming threat of an ecological catastrophe; the inappropriateness of the notion of private property in relation to so-called "intellectual property"; the socioethical implications of new techno-scientific developments (especially in biogenetics); and, last but not least, the creation of new forms of apartheid, new Walls and slums. There is a qualitative difference between this last feature - the gap that separates the Excluded from the Included - and the other three, which designate different aspects of what Hardt and Negri call the "commons;" the shared substance of our

social being, the privatization of which involves violent acts which should, where necessary, be resisted with violent means.[3]

If the reference to the commons justifies the return to the concept of communism, then the first three antagonisms should be read from the perspective of the fourth. Otherwise, as Žižek notes, "the first three effectively concern questions of humanity's economic, anthropological, even physical, survival, while the fourth one is ultimately a question of justice."[4] The risk is then to avoid the liberal appropriation of the concept of the commons, to resuscitate it from vague notions such as solidarity, or the common good, and similar political and conceptual sophisms. The enclosure of the commons results in a process of proletarization, which certainly goes beyond the social reality imagined by Marx.[5]

This brings us to a set of interrelated problems and questions. First, it concerns the function of philosophy in articulating the contemporary present. It might not be much of an exaggeration to boldly claim that this problem is at the same time the problem of philosophy itself. Namely, philosophically, thinking begins with and equals the attempts to articulate the present moment – just as Plato, in his *Republic*, tried to think of a city that would give people the best conditions to become philosophers. This was done based on the presupposition of philosophy of the equivalences of intelligences. The same applies to Hegel, who, in *Philosophy of Right*, does not try to outline the vision of a new state. However, even though one can assume the same premises of both Plato and Hegel, one crucial difference nonetheless stands between them. Unlike Hegel, Plato did outline and imagine an ideal state (going as far as to advise Dionysius on implementing a certain political idea), whereas Hegel was "content" with limiting himself to the analysis of the present. But, what is the connection between proletarization and philosophy? The proletarian position is defined as the moment when the worker is desubjectivized, rendered into a position equivalent to the money he receives for selling his labor power. In this sense, the proletarian position epitomizes the deadlocks generated by the antagonisms of capitalism.

Second, it concerns the interdependent relation between Marxism and philosophy, and communism and politics. When we speak of Marx and philosophy, do we speak of a relation between two different positions within the same discipline of thought, or do we have in mind two distinct intellectual disciplines, which do not exist and operate in the same register, but nonetheless are interdependent but intercorrelated with one another? The paradoxical thesis thus runs as follows: Marx (and Marxism) is not a philosopher (respectively, a philosophy); it doesn't occupy a position within philosophy. However, Marxism (understood here as a critique of political economy) has determining consequences for philosophy itself.

This leads us to the thread of the present chapter: what is the relation between philosophy and capitalism? Philosophy has always had an interest in capitalism, although capitalism has no interest in philosophy. Can, then, philosophy be of help in, first, understanding and, second, critiquing and eventually doing away with capitalism? It is not difficult to declare capitalism as a non-philosophical, if not an anti-philosophical, enterprise. It is non-philosophical because capitalism as a social system of production has abandoned its philo-sophical ambitions by claiming itself to be utilitarian. However, this is the ideological "truth" of capitalism: placing itself as the only social system which "works," which in turn reflects the success of capitalism, it pre-sents itself in neutral terms. Nevertheless, one has to point out some specificities, specific of capitalism itself. It is the first "system based on relations of domination" in which domination is out in the open, displayed, with no transcendental excuses. Just as Karl Marx points out in *The Communist Manifesto*:

> The bourgeoisie, wherever it has got the upper hand, has put an end to all feudal, patriarchal, idyllic relations. It has piti-lessly torn asunder the motley feudal ties that bound man to his "natural superiors," and has left remaining no other nexus between man and man than naked self-interest, than callous "cash payment." It has drowned the most heavenly ecstasies of religious fervour, of chivalrous enthusiasm, of philistine sentimentalism, in the icy water of egotistical calculation. It has resolved personal worth into exchange value, and in place of the numberless indefeasible chartered freedoms, has set up that single, unconscionable freedom – Free Trade. In one word, for exploitation, veiled by religious and political illusions, it has substituted naked, shameless, direct, brutal exploitation.[6]

In capitalism, people are obliged to see social relations for how they appear to be. There is no beyond, as it were – the domination and exploitation are based precisely in the appearance of the appearance. They do not take place in another, separate ontological realm. Following this logic, we could also argue that the openness, or the visibility, of domination in capitalism is precisely the visibility of the domination that makes it opaque. Here we can refer to the commodity form: although it is very clear that commodities do not have the attributes inscribed to them, only through a dialectical analysis can one show how they are nonetheless treated as if they had them. Therefore, it is only by means of a dialectical analysis that the trivialities (of the commodity form, relations of domination, etc.) become a true riddle of a given social form.

To return to the above-quoted paragraph from *The Communist Manifesto*, in capitalism, there is a sense in which capitalism makes us think. The strangeness of our situation is that despite capitalism being the form of organization of societies at the global level, we might not have the conceptual/philosophical tools to think it. But, just as Marx knew, capitalism is paradoxical in this respect: it is invisible, but at the same time the most thinkable of hitherto social systems (as no unthinkable God is relied upon to guarantee it).

Let us return to the famous line from *The Communist Manifesto*: "all that is solid melts into air." One possible thesis would be to argue that most of (contemporary) philosophies haven't lived up to capitalism yet, not in the sense of being able to stand up to capitalism itself, but in the sense of not fully accepting the full extent and consequences of the statement from the *Manifesto*. In a sense, they usually cling to some solidity. Philosophy does not think capitalism. However, capitalism is a problem that concerns philosophy, insofar as philosophy, broadly speaking, is founded on an Idea that is in its "nature" anti-capitalistic. Thus philosophy can be said to be properly contemporary if it accepts the consequences and the implications of all that is solid melts into air. The solid appears in many forms, from religion, to technology, to return to the premodern forms of social organization of society – and the list goes on. The sacred, which the force of capital so ruthlessly destroys and replaces with the icy force of the market, is in fact the compensation that tries to cover up for the perpetual rupture and breaks caused by capitalist relations. Needless to say, it is a reactionary compensation.

Therefore, the supplementary thesis should be that it is an odd supposition to claim that capitalism is a non-philosophical system. It is odd, because capitalism is the most abstract-based system of social organization in the history of humanity. Let us take the example of financial capital. Marx's classic formula of M-C-M (money-capital-money) seems to be transformed into M-M. That is to say, the valorization is bypassed and money is bought by money itself, without the commodity as a mediating instance. But, is this really the case, where the physical level (dimension) of production is elevated into the metaphysical one (financial speculations, devoid of the ontic dimension, etc.)? I would argue that financial capital reorganizes the productive level, but not by bypassing it. The best example would be that of great events like the Olympics or the FIFA World Cup, which are productive (in a new way) events, but which only make sense from the standpoint of the financial circuit of international capital. In *Grundrisse*, Marx argues that, in capitalism,

> objective dependency relations also appear, in antithesis to those of personal dependence (the objective dependency relation is nothing more than social relations which have become independent and now enter into opposition to the seemingly independent individuals; i.e. the reciprocal

relations of production separated from and autonomous of individuals) in such a way that individuals are now ruled by abstractions, whereas earlier they depended on one another. The abstraction, or idea, however, is nothing more than the theoretical expression of those material relations which are their lord and master.[7]

It is these relations that then can be expressed

> only in ideas, and thus philosophers have determined the reign of ideas to be the peculiarity of the new age, and have identified the creation of free individuality with the overthrow of this reign. This error was all the more easily committed, from the ideological stand-point, as this reign exercised by the relations (this objective dependency. which, incidentally, turns into certain definite relations of personal dependency, but stripped of all illusions) appears within the consciousness of individuals as the reign of ideas, and because the belief in the permanence of these ideas, i.e. of these objective relations of dependency, is of course consolidated, nourished and inculcated by the ruling classes by all means available.[8]

The word "Idea" should be understood in its Hegelian sense. In the preface to his *Philosophy of Right*, Hegel writes: "what is rational is actual; and what is actual is rational."[9] This thesis is (one of many other) reasons why his reputation suffers so greatly even to this day. According to his critics, this statement is meant to justify the Prussian monarchy, and thereby closes up the possibility for change, transformation, and revolution of the contemporary present. Further, it is also read as a reconciliation of thought/thinking with the present state of things, which therefore means abandoning any attempt to think and change both the present political order, as well as the present state of thinking. Thus, with "real is rational and rational is real," Hegel would have arrived at the absolute of philosophy, politics, history, etc. However, what he is arguing for is the opposite: he clearly states that going away from the "ideal" and defending reason as part of the real means saying that everything is "subject to sway of chance" and to "decay and corruption" – it is a way of preventing us from saying that when we think things in their being we are protecting them from contingency; philosophy accepts that eternity is at stake in history, but nothing in history is eternal.

> Before the pure light of this divine Idea – which is no mere Ideal – the phantom of a world whose events are an incoherent concourse of fortuitous circumstances, utterly vanishes. Philosophy wishes to discover the substantial purport, the real side, of the divine idea, and to justify the so much despised Reality of things; for Reason is the comprehension of the Divine work. But as to what concerns the perversion, corruption, and ruin of religious, ethical, and moral purposes, and states of society generally, it must be affirmed that in their essence these are infinite and eternal; but that the forms they assume may be of a limited order, and consequently belong to the domain of mere nature, and be subject to the sway of chance. They are therefore perishable, and exposed to decay and corruption.[10]

The crucial thesis here is the immanent existence of ideas outside of themselves: "nothing is actual except an idea."[11] Herein comes the normative dimension of the Hegelian idea. The relation between philosophy and critique is, as Hegel knew, very important – a paradoxical position, given that Hegel wasn't a critical thinker. However, it is both critique and philosophy that are threatened today, precisely because they lack the conceptual framework within which they can articulate themselves or enact their operation as activities of thought. Lacking the conceptual framework, both critique and philosophy become sterile and obsolete, degrading merely into an articulation of opinions. It might be that we need Hegel today more than ever precisely because he was the critical philosopher with no critique – immanent critiques are all about how systems criticize themselves, not about engaging with them from without. Perhaps this is a good reason why Marx, a materialist, could only adopt the Hegelian method when thinking of capitalism: it is the only method which, abandoning the critical standpoint (which capitalism overtly takes toward itself already), is still able to "carve out" some indetermination in history.

The big social, scientific, political, and economic transformations of recent decades have reaffirmed the need to return to the critique of political economy as the condition for every possible form of communist politics. Can Marx's work give us an idea of the contemporary form of capitalist development? Or, differently put, does Marx's work provide the conceptual framework within which to think about the transformations of capitalism? Earlier we spoke of the possible definition of the contemporaneity of philosophy. But when we discuss Marx's critique of political economy, by which principle do we measure the contemporaneity of his theory? Many have argued that Marx's theory is a cornerstone for rethinking both the critique of political economy and the effects of the transformation of capitalism. The obstacle concerns the analysis of (among other) dimensions of forms of social domination and exploitation, profit versus rent, social relations under contemporary capitalism, its dynamics, and so on.

The aim of this chapter is thus to propose a return to Marx, by way of rethinking the labor theory of value and exploitation.

Dialectics for Marx

The approach to a critique of political economy, insofar as it does not regress into what Althusser called "economist deviation," has to be grounded in (or, at least mediated by) a philosophical position. Taken in isolation and studied as an object in-itself, the epistemological status of the critique of political economy, and especially of capital, becomes obscure. When we spoke of Marx's relation with philosophy, we argued that his critique of political economy doesn't fall into the field of philosophy. However, it is interesting to analyze the way and the form in which Marx employs the concept of critique in his entire opus. He begins with a critique of religion, thus elevating it to the head of all criticism ("the criticism of religion . . . is the prerequisite of all criticism"); he continues with a critique of philosophy ("philosophy and the study of the actual world have the same relation to one another as onanism and sexual love."); and ends, finally, with a critique of political economy. This all seems to be circular, because Marx's critique of political economy brings him back to the critique of religion. More precisely, the famous subsection of the first chapter of *Capital*, on commodity fetishism, evokes the religious structure of the commodities, albeit at two different "levels" – that is, religion being a phenomenon that belongs to the superstructure, while commodity fetishism pertains to the economic base. Here we can advance by provisionally defining philosophy as a discipline of objectless knowledge, which should not be understood as an organized theoretical body of knowledge production, thus limiting it only within the epistemological horizon of itself; philosophy should be understood and conceptualized in ontological presuppositions. Philosophy, as Althusser argues, has no object of its own; it has itself as one of the fields of its preoccupation. On the other hand, a critique of political economy has itself as its own object insofar as the object of its study is not understood as a theoretical mutation of classical political economy, at the level of object, method, and theory.

This poses the fundamental question regarding Marx's late work, that is, the philosophical grounds within which the critique of political economy can rethink its presuppositions, the present, etc. The theorist who has undertaken one of the most serious and challenging reinterpretations of Marx's late work is Moishe Postone. His project consists of "reformulating a powerful critical theory of capitalism."[12] In this part, I shall deal with only one specific of his work, that is, his understanding of dialectics in the relation between Hegel and Marx.[13] In his reading of Marx's relation to Hegel, Postone offers a historical trajectory of Marx's rejection and approval of Hegel. This analysis tries to sort out the levels in which Marx's conceptualization of capital is indebted to Hegel's Spirit, Subject qua Substance, totality, etc.

The conclusion concerning dialectical method at which Postone arrives should be cited at length:

The structure of the dialectical unfolding of Marx's argument in *Capital* should be read as a metacommentary on Hegel.

Marx did not "apply" Hegel to classical political economy but contextualized Hegel's concepts in terms of the social forms of capitalist society. That is, Marx's mature critique of Hegel is immanent to the unfolding of the categories in *Capital* – which, by paralleling the way Hegel unfolds these concepts, implicitly suggests the determinate sociohistorical context of which they are expressions. In terms of Marx's analysis, Hegel's concepts of dialectic, contradiction, and the identical subject-object express fundamental aspects of capitalist reality but do not adequately grasp them. Hegel's categories do not elucidate capital, as the Subject of an alienated mode of production, nor do they analyze the historically specific dynamic of the forms, driven forward by their particular immanent contradictions.

However, what Hegel does, according to Postone is that he asserts the *Geist* as the Subject and, for him, dialectics has the nature of the universal law of motion. On the other hand,

> Marx implicitly argues that Hegel did grasp the abstract, contradictory social forms of capitalism but not in their historical specificity. Instead, he hypostatized and expressed them in an idealist way. Hegel's idealism, nevertheless, does express those forms, even if inadequately: it presents them by means of categories that are the identity of subject and object, and appear to have their own life. This critical analysis is very different from the sort of materialism that would simply invert these idealist categories anthropologically; the latter approach does not permit an adequate analysis of those alienated social structures characteristic of capitalism which do dominate people and are indeed independent of their wills.[14]

As opposed to Althusser, who argues that Marx's materialism is not a mere inversion of Hegel's idealist system, but instead represents the material explanation of idealism's imaginary thesis, Postone argues that Marx's position vis-à-vis Hegel is not that of reversal or an inversion of its idealism into materialism, but that it represents its materialist "justification." He then takes a step further:

> *Capital*, then, is a critique of Hegel as well as of Ricardo – two thinkers who, in Marx's opinion, represented the furthest development of thought that remains bound within the existent social formation. Marx did not simply "radicalize" Ricardo and "materialize" Hegel. His critique – proceeding from the historically specific "double character" of labor in capitalism – is essentially historical. He argues that, with their respective conception of "labor" and the *Geist*, Ricardo and Hegel posited as transhistorical, and therefore could not fully grasp, the historically specific character of the objects of their investigations. The form of exposition of Marx's mature analysis, then, is no more an "application" of Hegel's dialectic to the problematic of capital than his critical investigation of the commodity indicates that he "took over" Ricardo's theory of value. On the contrary, his argument is an immanently critical exposition that seeks to ground and render plausible the theories of Hegel and Ricardo with reference to the peculiar character of the social forms of their context.[15]

This is what Postone calls "traditional Marxism," which is a "critical Ricardo–Hegel synthesis." His emphasis is on the concept of labor, which, according to that understanding of Marxism, is presupposed as a transhistorical source of wealth, but, at the same time, it is posited as a substance of the Subject. In capitalism, according to Postone's understanding of "traditional Marxism," social relations are conceptualized as obstructing the Subject from self-realization. Labor is what constitutes the totality, which is posited as the standpoint of the critique, whilst Marx's dialectic goes through a transformation from a historically specific movement, into an articulation or assertion of the practice of making history. Accordingly, the understanding of proletariat as Subject means that the activity which constitutes the Subject is to be fulfilled, and not overcome. This approach then makes it impossible to see this activity as alienation. Postone argues that every critique which is based on labor also maintains that "alienation must be rooted outside of labor itself, in its control by a concrete Other, the capitalist class."[16]

Thus, in Postone's understanding, if we conceptualize Marxism as the Ricardo-Hegelian, it ends up being a critique whose aim is "unmasking."[17] Although not dismissing the process of "unmasking" entirely, but aiming to go behind it, Postone's aim is to show that a Marxist critique, while including it in itself, does so only as a moment of a more "fundamental theory of the social and historical constitution of the ideals and reality of capitalist society."[18]

So, how are we to sum up Postone's position? He rejects the idea that proletarian labor is the source of emancipation; for him, far from being the principal point, labor is the main barrier of proletarian emancipation. Rejecting the thesis that "the source of wealth is labor," Postone maintains that labor is conceived such that it

has an abstract, impersonal, quasi-objective character. This form of mediation is structured by a historically determinate form of social practice (labor in capitalism) and structures, in turn, people's actions, worldviews, and dispositions. Such an approach recasts the question of the relation between culture and material life into one of the relation between a historically specific form of social mediation and forms of social "objectivity" and "subjectivity." As a theory of social mediation, it is an effort to overcome the classical theoretical dichotomy of subject and object, while explaining that dichotomy historically.[19]

Differentiating between two approaches to Marx's mature work, Postone distinguishes between a critique of capitalism "from the standpoint of labor" and a "critique of labor in capitalism," while taking the latter as the premise of his interpretation of Marx. In doing so, Postone argues that "the social relations and forms of domination that characterize capitalism, in Marx's analysis, cannot be understood sufficiently in terms of class relations, rooted in property relations and mediated by the market,"[20] but it is the analysis of commodities and capital which is in fact the analysis of the fundamental social relations in capitalism.

I would argue that this conceptualization of Postone's reading of Marx is based on his understanding of dialectics. In a review of Martin Niclaus's introduction to his translation of Marx's *Grundrisse*, Postone, together with Helmut Reinicke, posits dialectics as a theoretical form that is historically restricted to the analysis of modern phenomena. They argue that there is a parallel between the commodities and dialectics, locating them at a given historical context. The reason Marx chose the commodity as a starting point of analysis is not only because the wealth of those societies in which the capitalist mode of production prevails presents itself as "an immense accumulation of commodities,"[21] which means that he wants to locate his analysis in a particular society, in a historically determined moment; he does so because he employs a dialectic which is a method that belongs to a particular society and a particular historical time. Thus Postone's position seems to assert that the dialectic was born with commodity production. Further, the object of dialectics is the social form in which the commodities are produced. However, Postone seems to reject dialectic as the "universally applicable method," or, differently put, dialectic is not the right expression of an indeterminate reality whose very nature is contradictory. Instead, the dialectic is a historically determined critical method, which, having risen with the appearance of the commodity form, is the only proper method by which to analyze the social form that is determined by the totality of commodities, along with its historically specific contradictions. The dialectic therefore appears as a form of theory (or rather, philosophy) that can (critically) analyze capitalism, or modernism as such, but which cannot do it from a non-capitalist or post-capitalist standpoint.

Thus, should we accept Postone's thesis, or simply dismiss it as historicist, a position that runs throughout his work? To answer in a fashion that is dear to Postone himself, we should say that he is both wrong (i.e., dialectic appears as such only with the modern turn, that is, the capitalist society) and right (the fact that if dialectic appeared with modernism it doesn't repudiate its transhistorical validity and pretentions). Of course, capitalism is a historical form of social organization, but not every social formation is restricted to that formation at the level of critical tools and concepts, as well as the site-specific theory of how products (material or not) remain tied to their sites of production.

Postone understands Marx's dialectics as being different from the Hegelian version, in the sense that the former is "expressive of capitalist relations," while the latter "expresses them self-consciously." Accordingly, the double character of Marx's dialectics thus consists in, first, understanding it as a critical epistemology according to which forms of thought are understood historically, where the critique emerges from the thing itself, that is to say the contradictions of the capitalist mode of production. In being such, it becomes a critique that aims at negating the capitalist social form. Second, because of its negative character, Postone argues that the most powerful dimension of the critique of political economy is its temporality, that is, its historical determination; it can exist only insofar as the bourgeois form of social organizations is the dominant form.

Postone's shortcoming is that he doesn't recognize the power of social forms. That is to say, social forms are more impotent to prevent eternity than Postone accepts. Because the logic of dialectics is historically connected to the logic of early capitalism, we can think of them together, and not because the logic of capitalism was the logic of the immediate history. When Postone says that the dialectic will disappear with the disappearance of capitalism, he therefore means that the epistemological form which gave rise to dialectics is overdetermined by its historical moment. However, this doesn't mean that the internal logic of dialectics is "historical" in the sense that things or phenomena appear in dialectics in the order they appear in history. Since dialectics is a product of the capitalist era and, as such, disappears as a cognitive tool with capitalism itself, it doesn't mean that the dialectical method works by displaying things in the order of their historical appearance.

Another dimension to this is the lesson of structuralism, according to which a historical development of a notion, concept, phenomena, etc. cannot be reduced to the special and temporal boundaries within which it was "produced." The whole point of the dialectical process, as Hegel knew, is that the present is never alone, in the sense that it always carries with it its own past, which, from the perspective of the present, is reconfigured as the past. This is the true Hegelian reading of the beginning of the *Manifesto*, which articulates history retrospectively: "the history of all hitherto existing society is the history of class struggles." From the perspective of capitalist society, the present rewrites and "creates" the past. This is how we should, in the Žižekian reconceptualization of Hegel, understand totality: the historical moment which is not only the present, but includes in itself the past, as well as the future. Totality means a concrete historical moment, from which the past and the future appear. This can also be discerned in the production and circulation process, with regard to value, which is nominally produced with the commodity in the process of production, but it is only actualized with the completion of the circle of circulation. The same can be said about capital itself: capital is a (Hegelian) Subject insofar as its principle takes up the role and the function of the mediating activity, but at the same time becomes an agent of this mediation of the commodity exchange. The entire exchange of commodities in the capitalist form, then, is the self-movement of capital. Here we have Hegel's notion of Subject, also as a Substance.

In *Grundrisse*, Marx gives an excellent elaboration of the dialectical matrix, which points to the principle of retroactivity:

> Bourgeois society is the most developed and the most complex historic organization of production. The categories which express its relations, the comprehension of its structure, thereby also allows insights into the structure and the relations of production of all the vanished social formations out of whose ruins and elements it built itself up, whose partly still unconquered remnants are carried along within it, whose mere nuances have developed explicit significance within it, etc. Human anatomy contains a key to the anatomy of the ape. The intimations of higher development among the subordinate animal species, however, can be understood only after the higher development is already known.[22]

It is only from the capitalist mode of production that we can retrospectively comprehend precursory modes of social organizations of production. Here is the Hegelian dialectic that made it possible for Marx to consider the nature of capital. It is in this sense that dialectics takes its non-teleological and (in Postone's terms) transhistorical character.

However, a few more remarks are in order here. Postone's argument that dialectics is a product of capitalist history and therefore is "wired" to show the historical evolution of the commodity forms, does not say that dialectics presents things in their historical chronological order. Postone's argument seems to be more sophisticated than it appears, because it presents them in a logical order. However, for him, it can only do this because it is the product of capitalists' own internal logic.

The problem with Postone's thesis the way I understand it is that he fails to understand Alfred Sohn-Rethel's double thesis concerning real abstractions. Postone is correct, I believe, in repeating Sohn-Rethel's first move, which goes something like this: yes, the categories of non-dialectical philosophy (the one, the eternal, and so on) were both within a precise socioeconomic situation, such as, for instance, the invention of coinage in seventh-century BC Ionia. Dialectical categories were equally conditioned by the new socioeconomic situation of capitalism. But, Sohn-Rethel also demonstrated that this "side-effect" of socioeconomic life lives on after that particular historical moment and it continues to be effective, just as those categories also gave birth to the modern scientific paradigm, as well as to the mathematical treatment of pure quantities, etc., which continue to be effective. The same logic should be applied to dialectics: yes, it is historically conditioned, but this does not mean that it becomes illusory once the historical conditions that gave birth to it are no longer there. It is my understanding that the second thesis is where the problematic dimension of Postone's thesis lies.

But, how are we to think about capital with Hegel? Who, to formulate it in a Žižekian fashion, could not see the very Hegelian dimension of the capitalist order, which was emerging right in front of him?

Hegel and Capitalism

Hegel is not particularly known as the philosopher critic of capitalism. He hardly ever mentions the word capitalism. Is his philosophical system merely a support of the existing system (that is, "what is actual is real . . ."), or did

he see immanent antagonisms constitutive of capitalism? In other words, is capitalism compatible with the
Hegelian ethical system? Differently put, is capitalism
compatible with the results of his thinking, or is there a
flaw in what he seemed to accept and the outcome of this
acceptance?

At this point, we should clarify the immanent critique
of Hegel, of which we spoke above. The way we understand it is that Hegelian immanency can exceed the
interiority of the present, that is to say, the present of the
concept to itself.

The usual criticism of Hegel runs something like this:
Hegelian speculative thinking runs from one concept to
another, thus leaving behind the reality. According to
this line of argumentation, Hegel reduced and deduced
nature, spirit, society, law, etc. from his logical categories,
so the concrete is produced out of the abstract universal.
Hegel, so the argumentation goes, committed the sin of
abstraction, which reverses the order of things, where
the process of "creation" begins with the concept, thus
replacing that of the concrete or the real. The partisan of
this thesis was Althusser, who accuses Hegel of the "bad
use of abstraction," that is, the speculative and idealist,
instead of the good and materialist, use of it. Surprisingly,
the image of Hegel as a monster was a point that united
both Marxists and non-Marxists, especially in France.
To paraphrase Derrida, Althusser along with Deleuze,
Foucault, and other French philosophers suffered from
an organized allergy against Hegel. Perhaps this is best
formulated by Deleuze, who argues that *"philosophy
since Hegel appears as a bizarre mixture of ontology and
anthropology, metaphysics and humanism, theology and
atheism, theology of bad conscience and atheism of res-*

sentiment."[23] This plague can be traced back to Kojève, whose reading of Hegel's *Phenomenology of Spirit*, and especially the absolute knowledge, left its traces in all of postwar French philosophy.

It was Marx himself who, in *Grundrisse*, summarized this position when he writes that:

> Hegel fell into the illusion of conceiving the real as the product of thought concentrating itself, probing its own depths, and unfolding itself out of itself, by itself, whereas the method of rising from the abstract to the concrete is only the way in which thought appropriates the concrete, reproduces it as the concrete in the mind.[24]

This rejection of Hegel is based on the identification of being with thought. But, is this true? Hegel is regarded as the philosopher whose work marked the culmination of German Idealism, a period in which capitalism was establishing itself as the dominant mode of production in Western Europe. Hence the parity of idealism, modernism, and capitalism emerged as one of the guiding threads elaborating on Hegel's relation to his own contemporary present. But, should one look into the monstrous system of Hegelian philosophy for foundations of the critique of capitalism? Contra Marx, as we said earlier, we should argue that Hegel is perhaps the most genuine contemplative philosopher, who never embarked on an ambitious project to change the world. We all know the famous passage from the preface of the *Philosophy of Right*: "When philosophy paints its grey in grey, a shape of life has grown old, and it cannot be rejuvenated, but only recognized, by the grey in grey of philosophy; the owl of Minerva begins its flight only with the onset of dusk."[25] This is Hegel's profound materialist thesis, which should be read alongside the one quoted above (real is actual; actual is real). Hegel's claim that the owl of Minerva sets out only in the dusk, at the end of a long day of engaging in social practices, asserts that thinking follows the events. It is for this reason that thinking or philosophy cannot look into the future. Marx's position is exactly the opposite and here we should, following Žižek, speak of a materialist reversal of Hegel. While Hegel identifies with (the German Idealist) thinking – the owl of Minerva – Marx all too quickly is on the side of the Gallic Rooster (the Coq Gaulois, the French symbol of revolution).[26]

Hegelian thinking, or, as Marx used to say "method of inquiry," should then be understood as a way of reconstructing in thought, or thinking, a certain reality and not an a priori creation of thought out of thought itself. This is what characterizes his whole philosophical project. Let us proceed further in examining Hegel's "method of enquiry." In his *Philosophy of Right*, he seems to have anticipated the critiques against him:

> This is not how we proceed, for we merely wish to observe how the concept determines itself, and we force ourselves not to add anything of our own thoughts and opinions. What we obtain in this way, however, is a series of thoughts and another series of existent shapes, in which it may happen that the temporal sequence of their actual appearance is to some extent different from the conceptual sequence.[27]

Hegel's position is the following:

> What we are dealing with here is the working out of this development; and in order for this working out of the determination of the particular from the idea to take place, and for cognitive knowledge of the universe or of nature to

develop, knowledge of the particular is necessary . . . When science is mature, it no longer begins from the empirical at all, although for it to come into existence science requires passage from what is singular, or what is particular, to the universal. Without the development of the sciences of experience on their own account, philosophy could not have advanced beyond the point that it reached among the ancients.[28]

What is the category that defines the modern age, according to Hegel? We should bear in mind that there are two subjective features and events constitutive of modernity: the French Revolution (where the new idea of freedom emerged) and Protestantism, that is to say, Luther (with the crucial belief that the subject only believes what it truly sees to be true). Nonetheless, on a different dimension, Hegel identifies property as the defining principle of modernity.

In other words, the social form of modernity is defined by property. But property exists in relation to contract, wrongs, and crime. The point here is not whether the category of property and its derivatives (contract and wrongs/crime) is the correct one from which to analyze the modern world, or whether it fits correctly into Hegel's general system for that matter. Nor should we try to find certain sections in his work that might help us in declaring Hegel a partisan of anti-capitalism. Although Hegel was uncertain about the ability of capitalism to create general satisfaction, he did defend inequality and egoistic behavior in civil society. This can be seen in his undoubtedly equivocal section on civil society, where he discusses the particular (the individual) and universality (civil society), and argues that, despite being separate in the field of civil society, they nonetheless exist in a state of conditional interdependency. The individual alone cannot satisfy his needs without the universal; civil society would do a better job in "absorbing the strength of the universal." But Hegel argues that, for the two to exist, one has to transform into the other: the particular (individual) is indulged in everything that brings him pleasure and satisfies his needs – it is a "contingent arbitrariness, and subjective caprice"; while the universal, qua civil society (which is the "world of appearance of an ethical idea"), "affords a spectacle of extravagance and misery as well as of the physical and ethical corruption common to both."[29]

But is the state, then, only a means by which civil society realizes the needs and desires of its subject? Marx believed that Hegel conceptualized his state as a controlling instance of civil society. Particular individuals do not accept or reject the state because it does or does not fulfill their needs and desires, but, rather, subjects accept the rational state insofar as its structure corresponds to their will. According to Dieter Henrich, Marx was unable to grasp Hegel's conception of the state, because he relied on the conceptual apparatus of the *Phenomenology of Spirit*, that is, "as soon as one employs the conceptual framework of the *Phenomenology of Spirit* as a vehicle for interpreting the *Philosophy of Right* (of the objective Spirit), the theory of the *Philosophy of Right* collapses, and diagnoses of Marx's type become possible."[30] Marx understands Hegel's notion of the state as an Absolute. However, in Hegel's *Philosophy of Right* there are clear passages in which he understands the role of the state (also) as having to control antagonistic tendencies in certain fields of life, including the economy. For instance, he argued that the rational aspect of property "is to be found not in the satisfaction of needs but in the superseding of mere subjectivity of personality. Not until he has property does the person exist as reason."[31] At the same time, Hegel defends the labor contract.[32] But there are certain features present in his work that are symptomatic of his whole philosophical system – one of them being the concept of rabble.[33] These can be said to be one of many other points in Hegel's system, which he tentatively elaborated, but wasn't aware of doing it.

The problem this raises is perhaps one of the main tasks of philosophers working and operating under the hypothesis of communism: how to account for a compatible relationship between freedom, institutions, and communism. Žižek made the first move in this area. His argument is that the "original sin" of modern emancipatory movements can be traced back to the "young Hegelian" rejection of the authority and alienation of the state,[34] and the solution to the above-mentioned issue can be settled if the contemporary communist movement and philosophers were to "re-appropriate the 'old Hegelian' typos of a strong State grounded in a shared ethical substance."[35]

This is what we shall try to do in what follows: namely, outline a Hegelian-inspired Marxist theory of labor.

Theory of Labor

In a paragraph in the *Philosophy of Right*, Hegel talks about "abstract labor":

The universal and objective aspect of work consists, however, in that [process of] abstraction which confers a specific character on means and needs and hence also on production, so giving rise to the division of labour. Through this division, the work of the individual [*des Einzelnen*] becomes simpler, so that his skill at his abstract work becomes greater, as does the volume of his output. At the same time, this abstraction of skill and means makes the dependence and reciprocity of human beings in the satisfaction of their other needs complete and entirely necessary. Furthermore, the abstraction of production makes work increasingly mechanical, so that the human being is eventually able to step aside and let a machine take his place.[36]

The immediate association of this is the work of Adam Smith, for whom one of the main distinctive characteristics of capitalism is the division of labor. It is already well known that Hegel was familiar with the work of Smith and with the new developments in political economy (as the references in the *Philosophy of Right* show), and his understanding of work and labor – which Fredric Jameson has named a handicraft ideology – certainly goes beyond the conceptualization of Smith.

Hegel argues that abstract labor is transformed into machines; that is, if we formulate it in contemporary terms, it is transformed into automation. This echoes Marx, who demonstrates that the production process "passes through a series of metamorphoses until it ends up as the machine or rather as an automatic system or machinery,"[37] which means that, at the same time, the nature and activity of the worker are transformed, as they are determined by the machines and not the other way round.[38] Marx refers to this as a "historical transformation of the traditional means of labour." In the *System of*

Ethical Life, Hegel makes a pertinent comment on the structure of the transformation of labor:

> The entire object in its determinate character is not annihilated altogether, but this labor, applied to the object as an entirety, is partitioned in itself and becomes a single laboring; and this single laboring becomes for this very reason more mechanical, because variety is excluded from it and so it becomes itself something more universal, more foreign to [the living] whole.[39]

He continues:

> This sort of laboring, thus divided, presupposes at the same time that the remaining needs are provided for in another way, for this way too has to be labored on, i.e., by the labor of other men. But this deadening [characteristic] of mechanical labor directly implies the possibility of cutting oneself off from it altogether; for the labor here is wholly quantitative without variety, and since its subsumption in intelligence is self-cancelling, something absolutely external, a thing, can then be used owing to its self-sameness both in respect of its labor and its movement.[40]

Can then we simply draw a parallel, or a line of continuation, between Hegel and Marx? Henrich argues that Marx's failure to properly read Hegel's real-philosophy consists in the fact that he didn't rely on the *Science of Logic*, with which the *Philosophy of Right* has the same notional structure. One has to accept this thesis, precisely because Hegel becomes Hegel when he dismisses, or rather overcomes, the distinction between ontology and metaphysics and assumes one is actually the other. His big Logic is the ultimate proof of this thesis.

A short detour might be of interest. Slavoj

Žižek deliberated on the possibility of writing the *Phenomenology of Spirit* of the twentieth century, which would unite "technological progress, the rise of democracy, the failed communist experiment, the horrors of fascism, the gradual end of colonialism."[41] Are all the events that happened in the previous century, "its numerous 'coincidences of the opposites' – the reversal of liberal capitalism into fascism, the even more weird reversal of the October Revolution into the Stalinist nightmare – not the very privileged stuff which seems to call for a Hegelian reading?"[42] Although my aim is far more modest, it is nonetheless interesting to make the claim on a less grandiose, but yet penetrating, issue regarding the *Phenomenology of Spirit*. Can we take a different step from Henrich and look for a Hegelian-informed Marxist theory of labor in *Phenomenology of Spirit*? Although Marx uses Hegel a lot, he did not adopt Hegel's theory of labor. Incorporating Hegel's theory of labor into Marx will necessarily have certain consequences: (1) it will only fill a gap and can only be presented in line with the rest of Marx's theory; (2) by including it, one has to revise other major concepts in the entire opus of Marx, and this enterprise changes profoundly the "nature" of Marx's work, such that he will not be easily recognizable thereafter.

One of the least understood passages from Hegel's *Phenomenology of Spirit* is the part at the end of the chapter on self-consciousness, on how the master–slave dialectic is "solved" by work. This is a passage that continues to bother and puzzle many philosophers, including Marx, Lukács, Kojève, Lacan, Lebrun, Žižek, and others.

But, let us proceed in the following manner. Let us cite a passage from the *Phenomenology of Spirit*, which will serve as the guiding thread. Here is the full passage, worthy of being cited at length:

[T]he formative activity has not only this positive significance that in it the pure being-for-self of the servile consciousness acquires an existence; it also has, in contrast with its first moment, the negative significance of fear. For, in fashioning the thing, the bondsman's own negativity, his being-for-self, becomes an object for him only through his setting at nought the existing shape confronting him. But this objective negative moment is none other than the alien being before which it has trembled. Now, however, he destroys this alien negative moment, posits himself as a negative in the permanent order of things, and thereby becomes for himself, someone existing on his own account. In the lord, the being-for-self is an "other" for the bondsman, or is only for him [i.e. is not his own]; in fear, the being-for-self is present in the bondsman himself; in fashioning the thing, he becomes aware that being-for-self belongs to him, that he himself exists essentially and actually in his own right. The shape does not become something other than himself through being made external to him; for it is precisely this shape that is his pure being-for-self, which in this externality is seen by him to be the truth. Through this rediscovery of himself by himself, the bondsman realizes that it is precisely in his work wherein he seemed to have only an alienated existence that he acquires a mind of his own. For this reflection, the two moments of fear and service as such, as also that of formative activity, are necessary, both being at the same time in a universal mode. Without the discipline of service and obedience, fear remains at the formal stage, and does not extend to the known real world of existence. Without the formative activity, fear remains inward and mute, and consciousness does not become explicitly for itself. If consciousness fashions the thing without that initial absolute fear, it is only an empty self-centered attitude; for its form or negativity is not negativity per se, and therefore its formative activity cannot give it a consciousness of itself as essential being. If it has not experienced absolute fear but only some lesser dread, the negative being has remained for it something external, its substance has not been infected by it through and through. Since the entire contents of its natural consciousness have not been jeopardized, determinate being still in principle attaches to it; having a "mind of one's own" is self-will, a freedom which is still enmeshed in servitude. Just as little as the pure form can become essential being for it, just as little is that form, regarded as extended to the particular, a universal formative activity, an absolute Notion; rather it is a skill which is master over some things, but not over the universal power and the whole of objective being.[43]

The idea that work imprints negativity onto things is a profound one and it contradicts our usual understanding of the logic of exteriorization (*entäusserung*) as the process through which consciousness recognizes itself in its exterior – which is what Hegel seems to be saying when he states that "the shape [of the worked thing] does not become something other than himself through being made external to him." But if work was a matter of recognition and harmony between the creator and his creation, then what is imprinted in the object would be the positive traits of self-consciousness, that which one can grasp about oneself and therefore can equally recognize in the products of labor. However, this process could not be capable of any "*aufhebung*" of the slave's condition: positively, the object commanded by the slave would be analogous to the slave himself, commanded by the lord. Work could only mean the dialectical overcoming of the lord/bondsman duality if it could recombine in a new way the otherwise exterior tension between lord and bondsman. So, in order to understand the logic of work in Hegel, we must briefly reconstruct the previous steps in this section of the *Phenomenology*.

We are all familiar with how Hegel demonstrates that the contradiction of desire is "realized" as the struggle for recognition between two desires. Desire is an impasse: we desire something, but in desiring this we are also determined by it. If we obtain what we desire, we risk ceasing to be that desire. In this sense, to desire a positive object is also to risk positivizing desire, and thereby losing it, ceasing to desire. Only by desiring another desire can I take as an object an equally negative object, and thereby assert desire in the quality it lacks; that is, only by desiring another's desire can desire fulfill its underlying desire, which is to remain desiring. But, to take another desire for an object means also to become the object of another – that is, to risk a different sort of positivity, the positivity of being an object for the other. This is what Hegel calls the "struggle for recognition": which of the two desires will be recognized as the negative pole – whose essence, determined by the negativity of its object, is desire itself; and which of the two will be positivized, its negativity turned into an existential, therefore inessential, quality? Hegel calls "lord" that desire which is able to remain desiring by fixing the negativity of the other desire as its object, and "bondsman" the desire which becomes itself an object, while being incapable of fixating an object. The slave's desire desires what the lord desires – it is object-less in this sense – but the lord desires nothing at all, only what the slave can desire in his place.

Neither of the two positions is now trapped in the previous contradictory tension – between being and not being desire; instead, a new tension arises out of the dismemberment of this inherent contradiction between two separate poles. The lord's desire is only possible because it has the slave for its object, which means that all its content is determined by the other, while the slave is only connected to this content as a desire because he occupies the position of mediator between the positivity of these objects and the negativity of the lord. This is where labor emerges, as a displacement of the relation between lord and bondsman onto the relation between the bondsman and the objects. What Hegel points out is that when the bondsman works on reality in order to adapt it to the lord's desire, this laboring imprints negativity onto the objects of labor, revealing that the negativity of the bondsman's desire can appear to him as negative in the products of his labor rather than as a positive object for the lord. This is why Hegel says that servitude and fear are necessary moments resulting in a new logic: it is not the positive expression of the human in the material that renders work a new medium for the slave's recognition; it is, rather, that the alienation of the slave in the master, his obedience, has prepared him to fully submit to the obedience to nature needed for things to take shape. It is this absolute obedience which turns the fear of the master into "respect" for the material; in other words, it turns servitude, the opposite of freedom, into a knowledge of material constraints, which is a means for freedom.

This is an essential point: the "emancipatory" character of this dialectical move is not that the slave becomes "his own master" insofar as he "masters" the objects which he transforms. The crucial point here is that the relative mastery of labor over the exterior world makes labor, and not the laborer, into the master of the object – so the mediation that had to go through the lord, in order that the slave could relate to himself as a desiring being, is now mediated by his own labor. In other words, there is not an "overcoming" of the alienation of the slave in the master, but a deepening of it, given that the lack of control one had over the master is now the lack of control one has over labor itself. Things are not formed as we choose, either because determinate material effects are only produced through determined activities, by respecting the constraints of nature, so to speak, or because creative or expressive work equally escapes our initial plans and intuitions. The triad relation remains constant: desire was internally divided between desire of something, desire to continue desiring, and the object of desire, which could not resolve this tension; then this contradiction of desire was split into two: the master remains as a desiring desire, the slave as a desire of something, but this something is forever changing, in order to please the master. Finally, desire loses both its moments, and passes onto the object itself, so we have labor as that which transforms the object, making it not-what-it-is, an object appropriate for desire, but the desiring subject, which desires an object that would not negate it, is no longer there. Instead, we have man, as a desire submitted to labor, which is the active pole of the triad, mediating the relation between desire, which desires otherness, and the object, which becomes other to itself.

What is truly crucial for us to note here is that Hegel's theory of labor as the furthest entry of the negative into things, their turning-other, shares fewer ontological commitments than Marx's early humanist theory of labor. In *Economic and Philosophical Manuscripts*, where he develops Feuerbach's theory of generic being into an active form of unalienated labor, Marx uses the category of labor as an operator which serves a series of different functions: (1) it offers a materialist principle of intelligibility for economic theory (in opposition to property relations); (2) it accounts for man's metabolic relation to nature (against any idealist essentialism); (3) it also accounts for men's relation to each other as a species (against the idea that a "second nature" is needed for men to relate). This concept of "generic being" is the heuristic principle against which the alienation proper to capitalist social relations can truly be measured and understood. While workers relate to their productions and between themselves in homogeneous fashion – products of labor reflect our plans for them, while also concerning mankind as a whole – property relations alienate us from our activities, from our production, and from each other. So alienation is opposed to exteriorization as the ontology of work. But this is not so in Hegel's view. For Hegel, as we just mentioned, it is work, and not the worker, who is a "master" of the products of labor – the activity of creation takes precedence over the creation and the creator. In this sense, Hegel empties out any fantasy that supposed, "beyond" capitalist social relations, a paradise of unalienated labor, in which we are constantly recognizing ourselves in our productions.

I want to propose that, following this, we might be able to start the hard work of outlining a theory in which work is equitable neither with concrete labor in capitalism, nor with abstract labor. Or better still, if we reject the concept of labor produced by capital, what is left of work as such? Can we do this and follow the argument in the "from Marx back to Hegel" hypothesis proposed and elaborated in length by Žižek? As we have seen, Hegel's conceptualization of labor is neither feudal nor capitalist. Instead, he developed a concept of work, an ontological construction of labor, which is constitutive, and not a social phenomenon. If, then, alienation is constitutive of labor, what must be surpassed from it?

Recall the Hegelian concept of "reconciliation." Reconciliation is not the process whereby the subject absorbs the substance, embodying it within itself. Reconciliation, as Žižek has demonstrated, amounts to a "redoubling of the two separations," that is, "the subject has to recognize in its alienation from the Substance the separation of the Substance from itself."[44] The opposite of this is not dis-alienation, with humanist Marxists being the partisans of this position: just society (social-ism, communism) consists in overcoming alienation, where the people will recognize themselves as active agents.

With Hegel, we are allowed to think of alienation as a right; that is, as the right to lose control over one's own production – in the precise sense that an inventor is subject to his own creation – which is a better orientation for political transformation than the question of abolish-ing alienation or alienating social activities altogether. It is in this sense that we should understand Žižek's firm proposition that communism should not be conceptual-ized and understood as the subjective reappropriation of the alienated substantial content. Here comes the notion of reconciliation again: we should unequivocally reject all attempts to understand communism (the just society) as the reconciliation of the subject with its (alienated) substance. Reconciliation itself is the acceptance of the loss. Hegel understands spirit as that which is in motion, a "process of proceeding from, of freeing itself from, nature: this is the being, the substance of spirit itself."[45] Therefore, spirit is not the reservoir of substance, which is then to be reappropriated; it is the process of freeing itself from itself.

Since, for Hegel, subjectivity and alienation are both fundamental, the whole question then boils down to: what is the problem with the specific form of alienation in capitalism? One of the ways to answer this is by suggesting that in the capitalist form of social organization of production we are alienated from alienation – that is to say, there is no material basis which promotes emancipatory experiences of alienation as such. Certainly, this doesn't happen on any meaningful or significant scale, such that it would shake the content of alienation in capitalism. The other way of understanding this would be to look at Lenin. There is a particular sign of this in Lenin's work, because he knew that militancy is labor. But, a "professional revolutionary" is his symptomatic phrase, which waits for a concept of "non-capitalist" labor that can account for militancy as work. This theory would allow us to overcome the debate on voluntarist militancy versus alienated work, since militancy is a form of work – it consumes time and requires discipline, without simply equating militancy and capitalist work forms.

It is perhaps through the premises of inclusion of Hegel's concept of estrangement into the general conceptualization of labor, that we can articulate the concept of "non-capitalist" labor, because what is truly at stake today is finding a place for the negative work in the Marxist theory of labor-value.

To Resume
(and not Conclude)

We want to end this book by, first, pointing out some possible consequences of the respective readings. They are mostly sketches for work that still needs to be done. We follow the order of the chapters as presented.

1. One of the difficulties in reading Marx today consists not so much in assessing the validity or the contemporaneity of his critique of political economy, as in reversing the very method of reading. Reading Marx in reverse means providing a reading in which Marx is taken to answer his critics – those who proclaimed his analysis to be irrelevant for our era. Such a contemporizing reading of Marx must be linked to the realization of one of his fundamental theses, namely that capitalism is already global, that the reality of capitalism has reached its peak. Why? Because one of the most fundamental Hegelian dialectical moves consisted in rendering visible the limits or/and inconsistencies which precisely (and sometimes only) appear at the very moment of the full realization of a certain notion. Since capitalism faces no outer threats

(a socialist block, for example), the threats to capitalism that do emerge come from within, from its internal contradictions. The question thus arises: what happens to a certain notion when it reaches its complete actuality?

To put it in a rather simplified manner, object-oriented ontology maintains and defends the autonomy of objects, regardless of the specificity of the relation in which they occur, be it human, natural, or other. This is part of the strategy to debunk human primacy. But, as the Marxist reading of such a position demonstrates, this is also the reason why there is neither place nor space for the subject in this theoretical orientation. In this sense, OOO maintains that a change can occur only when there is a disruption from the outside in the configuration of objects. The problem with OOO is that its ontological premises seek either to supplement or to replace modern science with a premodern form of how things really are in themselves. Some of the representatives employ the Lacanian "formula of sexuation" to articulate the difference between modern metaphysics (qua the masculine side of universality) and OOO (qua the feminine side of non-all). In the latter, all things exist as objects on the same ontological level. In this sense, humans are only one of the elements, in the assemblage of things. But by too swiftly not only identifying the human with just another subject but also identifying the human with the subject, the inhuman core of subjectivity as such is lost from view (as depicted inter alia not only by Hegel and psychoanalysis, but also by Descartes). In OOO, there is no space for the subject, or subjectivity, because the subject is not an agent amongst others, but is crucially a gesture of passivization, and thus escapes the grip of OOO wherein one finds a reversal of one of the crucial legacies of Lacan: of structures with subjectivity, with an element that is constitutive but excluded from the structures. The Marxist reading of OOO thus demonstrates the need for a certain Cartesian element (subjectivity) in contemporary thought (and even Lacan was certainly a Cartesian, albeit a peculiar one) – of which Marx was fully aware.

But, the Hegelian-Lacanian answer to the mediation of objects and subjects is far more pertinent. This tension is resolved into a different level, that is, the object as such is inaccessible: every attempt to grasp it, locate it, seize it ends up in certain antinomies. The object can be understood not by way of clearing up the epistemological obstacles, but by seeing through them.

2. Reading Marx's analysis of the reduction constitutive of capitalist economy in line with Plato's allegory of the cave forces us to confront surprising consequences: not only is the previously assumed subject of history also but one of the shadowy productions of the cave system; in addition, this immediately complicates the question of what it would mean to exit the cave, the fundamental problem of liberation. Why is this a problem? Heidegger, in his reading of Plato's allegory, distinguished "different dwelling places"[1] through which the different subjects of the allegory must pass on their path to liberation. The first is where they live enchained in the cave; but the true question and problem occurs when the chains are taken off, since the "imprisoned are now free in a certain sense,"[2] but they nonetheless adhere to the shadows. This is because "[a]s long as one encounters nothing but shadows, these hold one's gaze captive,"[3] So, how to free the prisoners from this peculiar libidinal attachment?

This only happens when a prisoner is "conveyed outside the cave,"[4] when he is forced out. This indicates the place of the (libidinal, but also epistemological, political, and in a sense ontological) function of a master, as depicted in psychoanalysis. It is a figure that neither tells me what to do nor whose simple instrument I could become, but who tells me: "You can! - what? Do the impossible."[5] The master, forcing one out, is the one "who gives you back to yourself,"[6] lets you "become who you are"[7] - and this clearly shows how liberation must inherently be connected to Plato's theory of anamnesis: a theory that indicates that one must remember what one never (consciously) knew.[8] The master just makes me affirm that "I can do this," without telling me what "this" is or who "I" am. A further intricacy arises precisely from this reference to the master in psychoanalysis. For does this mean that the prisoners are in the position of the analysand? And if so, should one not here also recall the basic fact that (in psychoanalysis) an analysand is constitutively a volunteer?[9] How can we conceive of the idea of volunteering to be forced out of the cave?[10] To answer this, we must unfold a dialectics of master and volunteer. It must be a dialectics because, to some extent, the master constitutes the volunteers as volunteers by liberating them from their previous unquestioned position so that they become voluntary followers of the master's injunction, whereby the master ultimately becomes superfluous.[11] But does capitalism itself not massively rely on unpaid and thereby structurally "voluntary" labor? In which case, there are volunteers and "volunteers" as well as masters and "masters." These need to be distinguished. For it might just be capitalism's "voluntary" work that produces the shadows to which we adhere. We thus have to conceive of a different way of volunteering, a way for which a different kind of master is needed. A dialectics of master and volunteer still needs to be developed for (and maybe from) a reading of Marx.

3. From the perspective of combining readings of Marx and Hegel, there is a further dimension: that of Hegel's well-known dialectic of slave and master in relation to Marx's thought. Perhaps this is one of the pillars of reconstructing Marx for our era. The aim is not only to return to Hegel (from Marx), thereby privileging Phenomenology over Logic, but to read Marx from Hegel's perspective. Or, differently put, what would Hegel have written had he read Marx's *Capital*? There is almost a consensus among philosophers, Marxists, and non-Marxists alike, that *Capital* was possible only after Marx had engaged with Hegel, and especially his *Science of Logic*. In many letters written to Engels, Marx himself admits this; among other things, he argued that his theory of profit had to be reformulated based on Hegel's *Logic*. However, many twentieth-century Marxist philosophers didn't see Marx as the originator of his own thought, but looked instead at Spinoza for a philosophy that corresponds better to Marx's critique of political economy. According to perhaps the most heroic anti-Hegelian philosopher of Marxism, Louis Althusser, Spinoza was the true and genuine predecessor of Marx.

Back to the dialectics of master and slave. The Hegelian theory of work clearly informed Marx's early critique of Feuerbach. The curious aspect, however, is that Marx borrowed the theory of the generic life from Feuerbach, but made it active by returning to Hegel's theory of work as a formative activity. However, the problem is that the leftist ideological conception of "workerism" is based on a "rough" reading of Hegel proposed by Marx himself: Hegel never suggested that – as Lukács later put it – work is a "teleological activity." According to Lukács, in the economic totality of capitalist production, every act of production represents a "synthesis of teleological work," but "is itself a teleological, i.e. practical, act in this very synthesis."[12] Therefore, for Lukács, the teleology of labor is the key element in understanding the kernel of Marxism, but also for the dialectical understanding and conceptualization of the world as such. Lukács's understanding of the emancipation of labor has to do with a return to an original form of praxis; it should become a process of perpetual self-creation, a conscious relation to its environment, which, in his later life, he called the ontology of social being. Lukács proposed a subversion of the previous relation, thus inverting the link between means and ends. For Hegel, as elaborated in chapter 3 of this book, work is just any activity that imprints negativity (its estrangement, more than its "exteriorization"). Therefore, the idea that workers are those who know what they are doing, who produce things that are made strange to them through private property, is an anti-Hegelian position.

To read Marx from Hegel's standpoint, the theory of labor opens up a space for identifying estrangement through work. As a result, we can shed new light on the critique of political economy, party politics, militancy, and so forth. Here, we are not only dealing with philosophical tricks or niceties, because the appropriate inscription of the negativity in the work of Marx has far-reaching philosophical and political consequences.

The philosophical reading, as presented in this book, takes its shape by proposing and bringing forward what perhaps will have been productive short-circuits between Marx (and the Marxist tradition) and three of the most important philosophers: Plato, Descartes, and Hegel. A Platonic Marx in the capitalist cave, a Cartesian Marx defending subjectivity against its enemies, and a Hegelian Marx conceiving of self-relating negativity as fundamental to labor. This does not lead to a new orthodoxy, obviously, but it might lead to unexpected reunions, maybe even to some that are so unexpected that they coincide with the first encounter. And sometimes, though not always, it is from unexpected encounters that one can build something new.

Notes

Introduction: Reading Marx: Unexpected Reunions

1 V.I. Lenin, *The State and Revolution* (Chicago: Haymarket Books, 2014), p. 41.

2 Lenin, *The State and Revolution*, p. 41

3 Cf. Giorgio Agamben, *Profanations* (New York: Zone Books, 2007).

4 Lenin, *The State and Revolution*, p. 41.

5 Lenin, *The State and Revolution*, p. 41.

6 Lenin, *The State and Revolution*, p. 41.

7 Lenin, *The State and Revolution*, p. 90.

8 Lenin attacked such a position violently – even though it explicitly recognizes the existence of classes and class struggle – by stating: "A Marxist is one who extends the recognition of the class struggle to the recognition of the dictatorship of the proletariat" (*The State and Revolution*, p. 70). Today, we might modify this claim: think of the recent victory of Trump in the US. Could this not be seen as a reactionary representation of bourgeois domination, finally claiming: "Look, there are no objective facts, but there is only a reality mediated

by class struggle. And this time, we won!" If those who are – traditionally – supposed to deny the existence of class struggle openly declare that there *is* class struggle (and one should be aware: *there is* class struggle!), they can no longer be criticized for stating that their position implies a class bias (and this even pertains to the criticisms of the idea of "fake news": could it not be said that this is a peculiar assimilation of the fact that there are no neutral facts in the realm of politics? This is obviously not meant as approval of Trump but as an indication that his "politics" assimilates something that previously had a possible emancipatory potential – and maybe it is thereby no surprise that Steve Bannon described himself as a Leninist, having turned "Lenin" into "Saint Lenin" before).

9 Cf. Alain Badiou, *The Rebirth of History: Times of Riots and Uprisings* (New York: Verso, 2012).

10 Cf. Frank Ruda, *Hegel's Rabble. An Investigation into Hegel's Philosophy of Right* (London: Continuum, 2011).

11 For this, cf. Agon Hamza, "The Refugee Crisis and the Helplessness of the Left," in *The Final Countdown: Europe, Refugees and the Left*, ed. Jela Krečič (Ljubljana: IRWIN, 2017), p. 175.

12 Louis Althusser, Étienne Balibar, Roger Establet, Jacques Rancière, and Pierre Macherey, *Reading Capital: The Complete Edition* (London: Verso, 2015), p. 12.

13 Althusser et al., *Reading Capital*, p. 12.

14 The difference between Marx's "critique of political economy" and classical political economy and economists has been outlined by Michael Heinrich, in his *An Introduction to the Three Volumes of Marx's Capital* (New York: Monthly Review Press, 2004), pp. 29–38.

15 Althusser et al., *Reading Capital*, p. 13.
16 Ernst Bloch, "Nachwort," in Johann Peter Hebel, *Kalendergeschichten* (Frankfurt am Main: Suhrkamp, 1965), p. 139.

Chapter 1 Marx Reads Object-Oriented-Ontology

1 Graham Harman, *Immaterialism* (Cambridge: Polity, 2016). Furthermore, I am leaving out of consideration the relationship between assemblage theory and other similar approaches (Bertalanffy's and Luhmann's system theory), and also Judith Butler's recourse to the notion of assemblage (she uses this term in the specific sense of assembling in public).
2 This description is shamelessly condensed from Martin Müller, "Assemblages and Actor-networks: Rethinking Socio-material Power, Politics and Space," quoted from http://onlinelibrary.wiley.com/doi/10.1111/gec3.12192/pdf.
3 Harman, *Immaterialism*, p. 114.
4 http://www.ibtimes.co.uk/quantum-entanglement-new-research-discovers-potential-problem-quantum-computing-development-1615114.
5 Art Hobson, quoted from https://arxiv.org/ftp/arxiv/papers/1204/1204.4616.pdf.
6 Benedict de Spinoza, *A Theologico-Political Treatise and A Political Treatise* (New York: Dover Publications 1951), p. 387.
7 Manuel DeLanda, *Assemblage Theory*, (Edinburgh: Edinburgh University Press 2016), p. 142.
8 Delanda, *Assemblage Theory*, p. 151.
9 Gilles Deleuze and Félix Guattari, *A Thousand Plateaus* (Minneapolis: Minnesota University Press 1987), p. 155.

10 DeLanda, *Assemblage Theory*, p. 151.

11 Harman, *Immaterialism,* 116–17.

12 John Caputo and Gianni Vattimo, *After the Death of God* (New York: Columbia University Press 2007), pp. 124–5.

13 Wang Lixiong and Tsering Shakya, *The Struggle for Tibet* (London: Verso Books 2009), p. 77.

14 See Ramesh Srinivasan, *Whose Global Village? Rethinking How Technology Shapes Our World* (New York: New York University Press 2017). Numbers in brackets refer to the pages of this book.

15 Harman, *Immaterialism*, pp. 122–3.

16 Peter Hallward, *Out of This World* (London: Verso Books 2006), p. 154.

17 Sheila O'Malley, quoted from http://www.rogerebert.com/reviews/the-strange-little-cat-2014.

18 Quoted from http://variety.com/2014/film/festivals/film-review-the-strange-little-cat-1201148557/.

19 Jane Bennett, *Vibrant Matter* (Durham: Duke University Press 2010), pp. 4–6.

20 One should always bear in mind the scientific strength of so-called "reductionism": is science not at its strongest when it explains how a "higher" quality emerges out of the "lowest" ones?

21 Gilles Deleuze, *L'Image-mouvement* (Paris: Minuit, 1983), p. 122.

22 Deleuze, *L'Image-mouvement*, p. 81.

23 Paul Broks, *Into the Silent Land. Travels in Neuropsychology* (London: Atlantic Books 2003), p. 17.

24 Furthermore, the notion of subject as one among objects-actants does not account for its own position of enunciation: where does the subject who deploys the OOO theory speak from? From what standpoint? This

theory obviously cannot be uttered from the position of one among objects.

Chapter 2 Marx in the Cave

1 Hans Blumenberg, *Höhlengleichnisse* (Frankfurt am Main: Suhrkamp, 1996), p. 18.

2 Sarah Kofman, *Camera Obscura: Of Ideology* (Ithaca: Cornell University Press, 1999), p. 19.

3 I am grateful to Lorenzo Chiesa, Rebecca Comay, and Michael Heinrich for remarks on previous versions of this chapter.

4 G.W.F. Hegel, *Lectures on the History of Philosophy, 1825-6*, vol. 3 (Oxford: Clarendon Press, 2006), p. 187.

5 Kolakowski claimed that any attempt to overcome mythical thinking implies a "version of the myth of the cave." Cf Leszek Kolakowski, *The Presence of Myth* (Chicago: Chicago University Press, 2001), p. 114.

6 Blumenberg, *Höhlengleichnisse*, p. 109.

7 I am here obviously referring to Lacan's famous claim that "truth has the structure of a fiction" – which does not at all mean that there is no truth. I will return to this.

8 Plato, *The Republic* (Cambridge: Cambridge University Press, 2000), 514a–b, p, 220.

9 Blumenberg, *Höhlengleichnisse*, p. 121.

10 In the cave, there is a "light from a distant fire, which is burning behind" the prisoners and what they see are "shadows cast by the fire on the wall of the cave in front of them" (Plato, *The Republic*, 515a, p. 220), when objects – "statues and other carvings, made of stone or wood and many other artifacts that people have made" (Martin Heidegger, "Plato's Doctrine of Truth," in *Pathmarks* (Cambridge: Cambridge University Press,

1998), p. 157) – are carried along an intermediary path also situated behind them but blocked by a wall such that they can only see the shadowy reflections of what is carried around and hear the voices of those who carry it

11 Heidegger, "Plato's Doctrine of Truth," pp. 164f.

12 Blumenberg, *Höhlengleichnisse*, p. 26.

13 Blumenberg, *Höhlengleichnisse*, p. 46.

14 Alfred Sohn-Rethel, *Intellectual and Manual Labour. A Critique of Epistemology* (London: Macmillan, 1978), p. xiii.

15 Michael Heinrich, *An Introduction to the Three Volumes of Karl Marx's Capital* (New York: Monthly Review Press, 2004), p. 76.

16 Jean-Jacques Rousseau, *On the Social Contract* (New York : Dover Publications, 2003), p. 1.

17 Cf. Giorgio Agamben, *Means without Ends: Notes on Politics* (Minneapolis: University of Minnesota Press, 2000), pp. 49ff.

18 Alfred Sohn-Rethel, *Geistige und körperliche Arbeit. Zur Theorie der gesellschaftlichen Synthesis* (Frankfurt am Main: Suhrkamp, 1972), p. 248; missing in the English translation, F.R.

19 Adorno suggested that Hegel can only be read experimentally. I attempt to extend this claim to the reading of Marx. Cf. Theodor W. Adorno, *Hegel: Three Studies* (Massachusetts: MIT Press, 1993), p. 145.

20 One version of this can be found in Peter Sloterdijk, *Bubbles: Spheres, Vol. I: Microspherology* (Los Angeles: semiotexte, 2011).

21 Ferenczi for example claimed that there is a "biological tendency which entices living species to return to the idle state experienced before birth," that is for

him, into a cave. Sandor Ferenczi, "Versuch einer Genitaltheorie," in *Schriften zur Psychoanalyse*, vol. 2 (Frankfurt am Main: Psychosozial Verlag, 2004), p. 333. That the return to a cave arises from external and not internal needs is Hegel's position: "People looked for protection in caves and lived there, and whole tribes had no other dwelling; and this arose from imperious necessity." G.W.F. Hegel, *Aesthetics. Lectures on Fine Arts*, Vol. II (Oxford: Clarendon Press, 1975), p. 648.

22 Karl Marx/Friedrich Engels, *The Communist Manifesto* (London: Pluto Press, 2008), p. 84.

23 Sohn-Rethel, *Geistige und körperliche Arbeit*, p. 248; missing in the English translation, F.R.

24 Mladen Dolar, "The Comic Mimesis," in *Critical Inquiry* 43 (Winter 2017), pp. 577, 574.

25 Things get more complicated if one takes into account that the realm of pure thought is also depicted – in Hegel for example – as "realm of shadows." Cf. G.W.F. Hegel, *The Science of Logic* (Cambridge: Cambridge University Press, 2010), p. 37. I will briefly return to this at the end.

26 Blumenberg, *Höhlengleichnisse*, p. 111.

27 Blumenberg, *Höhlengleichnisse*, pp. 117, 102.

28 Alain Badiou, *D'un Désastre obscur. Sur la fin de la vérité de l'Etat* (Paris: Aube, 1998), p. 52ff.

29 Blumenberg, *Höhlengleichnisse*, p. 113.

30 For why this has an effect, especially on younger people, cf. Alain Badiou, *The True Life* (Cambridge: Polity, 2017).

31 This has been analyzed repeatedly by Slavoj Žižek as what he calls "Western Buddhism." Cf. Slavoj Žižek, "From 'Western Marxism' to 'Western Buddhism'," in

Cabinet 2 (Spring 2001), at http://www.cabinetmaga zine.org/issues/2/western.php.

32 Jacques Rancière, "The Concept of Critique and the Critique of Political Economy: From the 1844 Manuscripts to Capital," in Louis Althusser, Étienne Balibar, Roger Establet, Jacques Rancière, and Pierre Macherey, *Reading Capital. The Complete Edition* (New York: Verso, 2015), p. 68.

33 Karl Marx, *The Poverty of Philosophy* (London: Martin Lawrence Limited, 1937), p. 66; translation modified.

34 Cf. Jean-Claude Milner, *Clartés de tous* (Paris: Verdier, 2011).

35 Heinrich, *An Introduction*, pp. 34f.

36 Karl Marx, *Capital. A Critique of Political Economy* (London: Penguin Books, 1993), p. 677.

37 Heinrich, *An Introduction*, p. 95.

38 Slavoj Žižek, *Living in the End Times* (New York: Verso, 2010), p. 190.

39 "All the notions of justice held by both worker and the capitalist, all the mystifications of the capitalistic mode of production, all capitalism's illusions about freedom, all the apologetic tricks of vulgar economics, have as their basis the form of appearance discussed above, which makes the actual relation invisible, and indeed presents to the eye the precise opposite of that relation." Marx, *Capital*, p. 680.

40 Sohn-Rethel, *Intellectual and Manual Labour*, p. 19. Even though it is important that the processes of abstraction and reduction I will examine in the following pages only take place in the exchange process.

41 Marx, *Capital*, p. 165.

42 Karl Marx, *Grundrisse. Foundations of the Critique of Political Economy* (Rough Draft) (London: Penguin, 1993),

43 Marx, *Capital*, p. 149.

44 Fredric Jameson, *Representing Capital: A Reading of Volume One* (New York: Verso, 2011), p. 69.

45 Michael Heinrich, *Wie das Marxsche Kapital lesen? Leseanleitung und Kommentar zum Anfang des "Kapitals"* (Stuttgart: Schmetterling, 2008), p. 193.

46 Marx, *Capital*, p. 999.

47 Ibid., 125; my emphasis. On this, cf. David Harvey, *A Companion to Marx's* Capital (New York: Verso, 2010), p. 15ff.

48 Marx, *Capital*, p. 772.

49 Marx, *Capital*, p. 769.

50 As Heinrich convincingly remarks about the functioning of capitalist societies: "*Capital* and "land" in capitalist society obtain magical abilities similar to those of wood or cloth fetishes in allegedly primitive societies. People in bourgeois society therefore live in an "enchanted" world, in which a "personification of things" occurs: the subjects of the social process are not people, but commodity, money, and capital." Heinrich, *An Introduction*, p. 184.

51 Karl Marx, *Capital. A Critique of Political Economy*, vol. 3 (London: Penguin, 1991), p. 969.

52 It is not that political economy is a mirror of the society it depicts; it is "not the reflection of real relations but that of a world already transformed, enchanted. It is the reflection of reflection, phantasm of phantasm" – and precisely therefore ideology. Kofman, *Camera Obscura*, p. 11.

53 Karl Marx, *A Contribution to the Critique of Political*

Economy, in MECW, vol. 29 (New York: International Publishers, 1987), p. 265.

54 Heidegger, "Plato's Doctrine," p. 165.

55 Blumenberg, *Höhlengleichnisse*, p. 142.

56 Karl Marx, *Economic and Philosophical Manuscripts*, in *Early Writings* (London: Penguin Books, 1992), p. 290.

57 One should also mention that if capitalism managed to universalize its model of labor, as for example Negri and Hardt have argued, the traditional distinction between the class in-itself (the objective class composition) and the class for-itself (that appears when it is organized and acts as a class) needs to be overcome in theory (as it already has been overcome in practice by the laboring conditions). For example, the rich investment banker or broker works as much as (maybe even more than) an ordinary factory worker. Cf. Michael Hardt and Antonio Negri, *Labor of Dionysus. A Critique of the State-Form* (Minneapolis: University of Minnesota Press, 1994). Already Marx claimed that any worker (not only factory workers) is reduced to this minimum, since "the normal wage is the lowest which is compatible with common humanity, i.e. with a bestial existence." Marx, *Manuscripts*, p. 283. This may be one of the reasons why even "today's world is exactly the one which, in a brilliant anticipation, a kind of true science fiction, Marx heralded as the full unfolding of the irrational and, in truth, monstrous potentialities of capitalism." Alain Badiou, *The Rebirth of History* (New York: Verso, 2012), p. 12.

58 Alain Badiou, Frank Ruda, and Jan Völker, "Wir müssen das affirmative Begehren hüten," in Alain Badiou, *Dritter Entwurf eines Manifests für den Affirmationismus* (Berlin: Merve, 2009), p. 56.

59 Rancière, "The Concept of Critique," p. 84.
60 Heinrich, *Wie das Marxsche Kapital lesen?*, p. 169.
61 Marx, *Capital*, p. 165.
62 Slavoj Žižek, "Welcome to the 'Spiritual Kingdom of Animals'," at http://blogdaboitempo.com. br/2012/09/18/welcome-to-the-spiritual-kingdom-of-animals-slavoj-zizek-on-the-moral-vacuum-of-global-capitalism/. Marx clearly states: "animals are not able to *exchange*" (Marx, *Manuscripts*, p. 373) and it is precisely this system of exchange (and production) that generates this type of reduction. There is a path from the system of exchange to the animal, but none from the animal to exchange.
63 For some aspects of this "societal process of reduction," cf. Heinrich, *Wie das Marxsche Kapital lesen?*, pp. 96ff., 102, 151.
64 Jameson, *Representing Capital*, p. 63.
65 Žižek, *Living in the End Times*, p. 183.
66 For an instructive account of Marx's enterprise and the concept of political economy, see Michael Heinrich, *Die Wissenschaft vom Wert: Die Marxsche Kritik der politischen Ökonomie zwischen wissenschaftlicher Revolution und klassischer Tradition* (Stuttgart: Westfälisches Dampfboot, 2001).
67 Heinrich, *Wie das Marxsche Kapital lesen?*, p. 13.
68 Žižek, *Living in the End Times*, p. 204.
69 Second nature is synonymous with habit. Later Marx defends a similar claim, when he states that the "expression of value common to all commodities" – namely money – is mainly "by social custom [*Gewöhnung*]" through habit what it is (Marx, *Capital*, pp. 158, 162).
70 Marx, *Capital*, pp. 285–6.
71 Marx, *Capital*, p. 286.

72 Marx, *Manuscripts*, p. 260.

73 Marx, *Capital*, p. 797.

74 In the *Grundrisse* Marx pointedly emphasizes that the abstraction depends on specific social conditions: "Not only the category, labour, but labour in reality has ... become the means of creating wealth in general, and has ceased to be organically linked with particular individuals in any specific form. Such a state of affairs is at its most developed in the most modern form of existence of bourgeois society ... Here, then, for the first time, the point of departure of modern economics, namely the abstraction of the category of 'labour', 'labour as such' ... becomes true in practice." Marx, *Grundrisse*, pp. 104f.

75 Marx, *Manuscripts*, p. 327.

76 Marx will later call this the "lifelong annexation of the worker to a partial operation," which grounds his "complete subjection to capital." *Capital*, p. 477.

77 Jameson, *Representing Capital*, p. 25.

78 Heinrich, *Wie das Marxsche Kapital lesen?*, p. 95.

79 G.W.F. Hegel, "Who Thinks Abstractly?" in *Hegel: Texts and Commentary* (New York: Anchor Books, 1966), pp. 113–18.

80 Two additions: (1) Abstraction always obstructs the insight into its own constitution. It is an imaginarily totalizing relation to its own particular condition of existence. This means that bourgeois political economy is an ideological construction. (2) This explains why money is abstract: as a general equivalent it is a particular commodity that only relates to all particular commodities by essentializing the form of particularity (commodities). There can be a further universalization of (the general operation of) the particularization of

particularities, when abstraction is again applied to itself, redoubled, and this *relation* is what Marx calls capital. This is why capital appears as money generating money (self-realizing value) and as an abstract relation to abstraction. In capitalism, all is reduced to the perpetuation of this operation.

81 Alain Badiou, *Qu'est-ce que j'entends par Marxisme?* (Paris: Les éditions sociales, 2016), p. 24.

82 Jameson, *Representing Capital*, p. 125.

83 G.W.F. Hegel, "Aphorismen auf dem Wastebook," in *Werke*, vol. 2 (Frankfurt am Main: Suhrkamp, 1986), p. 552.

84 Alain Badiou, *Logics of Worlds. Being and Event, 2* (London: Continuum, 2009), p. 2.

85 Marx, *Manuscripts*, p. 328.

86 Marx, *Manuscripts*, p. 352.

87 David Harvey, *The Limits to Capital* (London: Verso, 2006), p. 161.

88 Marx, *Manuscripts*, p. 285.

89 Gilbert Simondon, *Two Lessons on Animal and Man* (Minneapolis: Univocal Publishing, 2011), p. 75.

90 Rebecca Comay, *Mourning Sickness. Hegel and the French Revolution* (Stanford: Stanford University Press, 2011), p. 117.

91 Sigmund Freud, *Introductory Lectures on Psycho-Analysis* (New York: Norton, 1989), p. 401.

92 Cf. Badiou, *The True Life*, pp. 50–73.

93 Luhmann used this notion to describe a type of organization (say an office) that is loosely linked to the people working in it (which is why for maintaining its operation it does not matter if the individuals working in it change). He argues that loosely coupled systems are more stable than tightly coupled ones. Luhmann,

Introduction to Systems Theory (Cambridge: Polity, 2012), p. 193.

94 Badiou, *Logics of Worlds*, p. 2.
95 Marx, *Capital*, p. 799.
96 Marx, *Capital*, p. 91.
97 Marx, *Capital*, pp. 289, 308.
98 Marx, *Manuscripts*, p. 329.
99 Frederick Engels, *Anti-Dühring*, in MECW, vol. 25 (New York: International Publishers, 1987), p. 98.
100 Karl Marx, *Critical Notes on "The King of Prussia and Social Reform. By a Prussian,"* in MECW, vol. 3, p. 206.
101 Marx, *Manuscripts*, p. 360; translation altered.
102 Marx, *Manuscripts*, p. 360.
103 Marx, *Capital*, p. 443. Not so long ago, George Akerlof (economics Nobel Prize winner in 2001) claimed that animal spirits – a wording made popular by Keynes in the 1930s – are what keeps capitalism progressing: cf. George A. Akerlof and Robert J. Shiller, *Animal Spirits* (Princeton: Princeton University Press, 2009).
104 Marx, *Capital*, p. 92.
105 Marx, *Capital*, p. 503. Marx later calls this the "encroaching [*übergreifendes*] subject" (*Capital*, p. 544; translation altered).
106 Marx, *Capital*, p. 544.
107 Heinrich, *An Introduction*, p. 111.
108 Jameson, *Representing Capital*, p. 113.
109 Marx, *Manuscripts*, p. 327; the last sentence is missing in the translation.
110 "[I]n a situation in which so little of life outside working hours remains," the only thing to do when not working is "sleeping" (Jameson, *Representing Capital*, p. 116) – when free from work, the worker sleeps his freedom away. Adorno gives this another twist: "Because people

have to work so much, in their free time they must quasi compulsively repeat the rituals of the efforts they are expected to do." Max Horkheimer and Theodor W. Adorno, "Diskussion über Theorie und Praxis" (1956), in Max Horkheimer, *Gesammelte Schriften*, vol. 19 (Frankfurt am Main: Fischer, 1989), p. 45. This is why people like to be productive and active in their free time.

111 "For a man who is starving the human form of food does not exist, only its abstract form exists . . . it would be hard to say how this way of eating differs from that of animals." Marx, *Manuscripts*, p. 353. Today the inverted claim might be even more true: the more one refines one's taste, the more one cares about what one eats, how it is produced, cooked, etc. the more abstract one's relationship to one own existence becomes.

112 Marx, *Capital*, p. 899.

113 Cf. Frank Ruda, *Abolishing Freedom: A Plea for a Contemporary Use of Fatalism* (Lincoln: Nebraska University Press, 2016).

114 G.W.F. Hegel, *Outlines of the Philosophy of Right* (Oxford: Oxford University Press, 2008), p. 33; translation modified.

115 G.W.F. Hegel, *Aesthetics: Lectures on Fine Art*, vol. 1 (Oxford: Clarendon Press, 1988), p. 80.

116 "[H]e does not know that he knows it and for that reason thinks he does not know." Freud, *Introductory Lectures*, p. 124.

117 Marx, *Manuscripts*, p. 328.

118 "What distinguishes humans from animals (the 'human animal' included) is not consciousness – one can easily concede that animals do have some kind of self-awareness – but the un-conscious." Žižek, *Less Than Nothing*, p. 824.

119 Marx, *Capital*, p. 1068.
120 "Light, air, etc. – the simplest animal cleanliness – ceases to be a need for man . . . Universal unnatural neglect, putrefied nature, becomes an element of life for him." Marx, *Manuscripts*, pp. 359f. Man is distinguished from other animals by the capacity to adapt to whatever extreme circumstances. Cf. Karl Barth, *Church Dogmatics, vol. 3: The Doctrine of Creation* (Edinburgh: T.&T. Clark, 1960), p. 115.
121 Badiou, *Logics of Worlds*, p. 114.
122 He is quite effectively less than nothing.
123 Marx, *Capital*, p. 135.
124 Cf. Karl Marx, *Value: Studies* (London: New Park, 1976).
125 When elaborating the concept of money, Marx famously quotes the "apocalypse," defining the relation between money and man: "These . . . shall give their power and strength unto the beast. And that no man might buy or sell, save that he had the mark, or name of the beast, or the number of his name." *Capital*, p. 181.
126 Marx pointed out that money "casts its shadow before it" into the future such that "it causes the commodity to move from the hands of the seller into those of the buyer." Capitalism is literally overshadowed by money. Cf. Karl Marx, *Outlines of a Critique of Political Economy*, in MECW, vol. 29 (New York: International Publishers, 1987), p. 373.
127 Marx, *Capital*, vol. 3, p. 205.
128 Marx, *The Poverty of Philosophy*, p. 102.
129 Žižek, *Less than Nothing*, p. 108.
130 Marx, *Capital*, p. 899. This is why "[t]he exploited consent to their own exploitation." Heinrich, *An Introduction*, p. 204. Since "[t]he reason for this reduc-

tion ... asserts itself as a regulative law of nature."
Marx, *Capital*, p. 168.

131 Heinrich, *Wie das Marxsche Kapital lesen?*, p. 211.

132 Marx, *Capital*, p. 135.

133 Cf. Frank Ruda, *Hegel's Rabble. An Investigation into Hegel's Philosophy of Right* (London: Continuum, 2001), pp. 75–99.

134 Hegel, *Outlines*, p. 159.

135 G.W.F. Hegel, *Philosophy of Mind* (Oxford: Oxford University Press, 2008), p. 131.

136 Cf. Slavoj Žižek, *Madness and Habit in German Idealism. Discipline Between the Two Freedoms*, at http://www.lacan.com/zizdazedandconfused.html.

137 Cf. Thomas Khurana, "The Potentiality of Habit: Notes on Self-Formation" (unpublished typescript).

138 Khurana, "The Potentiality of Habit."

139 Khurana, "The Potentiality of Habit."

140 Hegel, *Outlines*, p. 191.

141 Marx, *Manuscripts*, p. 360.

142 Marx, *Critical Notes on "The King of Prussia and Social Reform,"* p. 406.

143 Hegel, *Philosophy of Mind*, p. 199.

144 Marx, *Manuscripts*, p. 377.

145 Marx, *Manuscripts*, p. 327.

146 For an "[e]nd ... is the concrete universal." G.W.F. Hegel, *Science of Logic* (New York: Humanity Books, 1969), p. 739.

147 Cf. Hegel, *Science of Logic*, pp. 711–34.

148 Hegel, *Science of Logic*, p. 736.

149 This interpretation of ends leads, for example, to an assumption that the freedom of the press is already emancipation and was rightly criticized as a confusion of means and ends, as "taking the shadow for the thing

and getting nothing." Cf. Friedrich Engels, "Deutsche Zustände III," in MEW, vol. 2 (Berlin: Dietz, 1962), p. 583.

150 Marx and Engels, *Communist Manifesto*, p. 37.

151 Marx and Engels, *Communist Manifesto*, pp. 38, 36, 45.

152 Marx, *A Contribution*, p. 264.

153 As becomes increasingly obvious today, capitalism works by regressing to previous forms of domination. Cf., for example, https://www.vice.com/en_us/article/4waq9n/the-slaves-of-dubai.

154 Rancière, "The Concept of Critique," p. 108.

155 "[T]he subject loses the substantial density which made it the constitutive principle of all objectivity, of all substantiality, retaining only the meagre reality of a bearer." Rancière, "The Concept of Critique," p. 106.

156 Cf. Peter Sloterdijk, *In the World Interior of Capital. For a Philosophical Theory of Globalization* (Cambridge: Polity, 2013).

157 Rancière, "The Concept of Critique," p. 86.

158 Rancière, "The Concept of Critique," p. 87.

159 For one contemporary attempt to actualize the theory of the turn(ing of the gaze) in capitalism's cave, cf. Alain Badiou, "De quel réel cette crise est-elle le spectacle?" at http://www.entretemps.asso.fr/Badiou/Crise.htm.

160 Hegel, *Phenomenology*, p. 103.

161 Marx, *Capital*, p. 174.

162 Hegel, *The Science of Logic*, p. 37.

163 Hegel, *The Science of Logic*, p. 29.

164 Alain Badiou suggested that a practice of truth has an effect on the constituted knowledge of a given situation (he calls this effectuation "forcing") that is similar to the return to the cave.

165 One also needs a peculiar kind of master (God) to be

able to do so: a master who does not help on any step of the way, as we are not simply finding out what he thought but quite literally doing all the work on our own.

166 Hegel, *Phenomenology*, p. 19.

Chapter 3 Imprinting Negativity: Hegel Reads Marx

1 I want to thank Gabriel Tupinambá, Frank Ruda, and Serene Richards for their comments on previous drafts of this chapter.

2 The use of the expression "late capitalism" might appear as paradoxical. Isn't it always conceptualized as *late capitalism*, starting from Lenin, , who famously said that imperialism is the highest stage of capitalism, to the German socialists of the 1930s, all the way to Fredric Jameson who designated the neoliberal form of capitalism as the late phase of capitalism?

3 Slavoj Žižek, *First as Tragedy, Then as Farce* (London: Verso, 2009), pp. 90–1.

4 Slavoj Žižek, *The Courage of Hopelessness: Chronicles of a Year of Acting Dangerously* (London: Allen Lane, 2017), p. xix.

5 Cf. Gabriel Tupinambá, "The Unemployable and the Generic: Rethinking the Commons in the Communist Hypothesis," *Palgrave Communications*, 3 (August 2017), at https://www.nature.com/articles/palcomms 201773.

6 Karl Marx and Friedrich Engels, "The Communist Manifesto," in *The Communist Manifesto and Other Writings* (New York: Barns & Noble Classics), pp. 9–10.

7 Karl Marx, *Grundrisse: Foundations of the Critique of Political Economy* (London: Penguin Books, 1993), p. 164.

8 Marx, *Grundrisse*, p. 165.

9 G.W.F. Hegel, *Elements of the Philosophy of Right* (Cambridge: Cambridge University Press, 1991), p. 20.

10 G.W.F. Hegel, *Philosophy of History*, (Ontario: Batoche Books, 2001), p. 51.

11 Hegel, *Elements of the Philosophy of Right*, p. 20.

12 Moishe Postone, "Labor and the Logic of Abstraction," *South Atlantic Quarterly*, 108/2 (2009), p. 307.

13 For a detailed critical reading of Postone's work, see Slavoj Žižek, *Living in the End Times* (New York: Verso, 2010), pp. 191–243.

14 Moishe Postone, *Time, Labor and Social Domination: A Reinterpretation of Marx's Critical Theory* (Cambridge: Cambridge University Press, 1993) p. 81.

15 Postone, *Time, Labor and Social Domination*, pp. 81–2.

16 Postone, *Time, Labor and Social Domination*, p. 82.

17 Postone, *Time, Labor and Social Domination*, p. 82.

18 Postone, *Time, Labor and Social Domination*, p. 83.

19 Postone, *Time, Labor and Social Domination*, p. 5.

20 Postone, *Time, Labor and Social Domination*, p. 6.

21 Karl Marx, *Capital: A Critique of Political Economy*, vol, 1 (London: Penguin Classics, 1990), p. 125.

22 Marx, *Grundrisse*, p. 105.

23 Gilles Deleuze, *Nietzsche and Philosophy* (New York: Columbia University Press, 2006), p. 183; emphasis in the original.

24 Marx, *Grundrisse*, p. 101.

25 Hegel, *Elements of the Philosophy of Right*, p. 23.

26 Slavoj Žižek, *Less Than Nothing: Hegel and the Shadow of Dialectical Materialism* (London: Verso 2012), p. 220.

27 Hegel, *Elements of the Philosophy of Right*, p. 61.

28 G.W.F. Hegel, *Lectures on the History of Philosophy*, vol. 3 (Oxford: Clarendon Press, 2009), pp. 89–90.

29 Hegel, *Elements of the Philosophy of Right*, p. 222.

30 Dieter Henrich, *Between Kant and Hegel: Lectures on German Idealism* (Cambridge, MA: Harvard University Press, 2008), p. 329.

31 Hegel, *Elements of the Philosophy of Right*, p. 73.

32 See Hegel, *Elements of the Philosophy of Right*, pp. 97–8.

33 For an excellent reading of this, see Frank Ruda, *Hegel's Rabble: An Investigation into Hegel's Philosophy of Right* (New York: Continuum, 2011).

34 Žižek *Living in the End Times*, p. 200.

35 Žižek *Living in the End Times*, p. 200.

36 Hegel, *Elements of the Philosophy of Right*, pp. 232–3.

37 Karl Marx and Friedrich Engels, *Collected Works, Volume 29* (New York: International Publishers, 1987), p. 82.

38 Marx and Engels, *Collected Works*, p. 83.

39 G.W.F. Hegel, *System of Ethical Life and the First Philosophy* (Albany: State University of New York Press, 1988), p. 117.

40 Hegel, *System of Ethical Life*, p. 117.

41 Žižek, *Less Than Nothing*, p. 225.

42 Žižek, *Less Than Nothing*, p. 226.

43 G.W.F. Hegel, *Phenomenology of Spirit* (Oxford: Oxford University Press, 1977), pp. 117–18.

44 Žižek, *Living in the End Times*, pp. 227–8.

45 Quoted from Žižek, *Living in the End Times*, p. 230.

To Resume (and not Conclude)

1 Martin Heidegger, "Plato's Doctrine of Truth," in *Pathmarks* (Cambridge: Cambridge University Press, 1998), p. 168.

2 Heidegger, "Plato's Doctrine of Truth," p. 168.

3 Heidegger, "Plato's Doctrine of Truth," p. 169.

4 Heidegger, "Plato's Doctrine of Truth," p. 169.
5 Slavoj Žižek, *Lenin 2017. Remembering, Repeating, Working Through* (New York: Verso, 2017), p. lxii.
6 Žižek, *Lenin 2017*, p. lxii.
7 Cf. Friedrich Nietzsche, *Ecce Homo. How to Become What You Are* (Oxford: Oxford University Press, 2007).
8 Cf. Frank Ruda, *For Badiou: Idealism without Idealism* (Evanston: Northwestern University Press, 2015), pp. 115ff.
9 Cf. Alain Badiou, *Lacan. L'Antiphilosophie 3 (1994–1995)* (Paris: Fayard, 2013), p. 101.
10 One answer might be given if one recalls the emancipatory potential of fatalism. Cf. Frank Ruda, *Abolishing Freedom: A Plea for a Contemporary Use of Fatalism* (Lincoln: Nebraska University Press, 2016).
11 And maybe this process of liberation has to be repeated over and over again to obstruct the formation of too stable a habit.
12 György Lukács, *History and Class Consciousness* (Cambridge, MA: MIT Press, 1972), p. xx.

Index

169

Index

immaterialism 23, 26

Jameson, Fredric 72, 128

Kant, Immanuel 48, 51, 58, 64
Kofman, Sarah 62
Kojève, Alexandre 123, 130

labor 11, 69, 73, 79–80, 82–83,
  88, 92, 102, 104, 111, 114–116,
  127–139, 143, 145–146
Lacan, Jacques 29–30, 36, 43, 46,
  54, 58–61, 130, 142, 151
Laclau Ernesto 22, 56
Lebrun, Gérard 130
Lenin, V.I. 4–7, 138
Lukács, György 130, 145

Marx, Karl 1, 3–8, 10, 12–17, 44,
  53–55, 65–74, 78–80, 82–83,
  85–86, 88–90, 92–93, 97–100,
  103–107, 110–116, 118, 120,
  123–124, 126, 128–130, 136–137,
  140, 142, 144–146
Marxism 1, 2, 4–11, 17, 55, 104,
  114–115, 144–145
master/slave 130, 132–135,
  144–145
master/volunteer 143–144
materialism 24, 25, 26, 113
mechanism 17, 18, 25, 91–96, 99
money 89, 93, 104, 107
myth 63, 97

naturalization 20, 64, 78, 86,
  89–90, 97–98, 102

object-oriented ontology (OOO)
  17, 24, 57, 61, 141, 142
objet a 56, 57

Plato 10, 14, 62–67, 71–72, 81,
  98–99, 103, 142–143, 146
Postone, Moishe 112–118,
  120–121
proletariat 6, 55–56, 81, 115

reduction 49, 71–77, 79, 81–84,
  86–89, 91–93, 142
Rousseau, Jean-Jacques 64
Ruda, Frank 10

Sohn-Rethel, Alfred 66, 121
Spinoza, Baruch 13–14, 30–31,
  144

teleology 49, 145
time/temporality 8, 33, 84, 90,
  97–98, 118–119, 124
totality 17–18, 43–44, 112, 115, 119,
  145

universality 23–24, 33, 35–37, 39,
  42–43, 53, 55–56, 76, 125, 141

Žižek, Slavoj 10, 35, 102–103, 121,
  124, 127, 129–130, 137